Money, Taste, and Wine

Money, Taste, and Wine

It's Complicated!

MIKE VESETH

ROWMAN & LITTLEFIELD
Lanham • Boulder • New York • London

Published by Rowman & Littlefield
A wholly owned subsidary of The Rowman & Littlefield Publishing Group, Inc.
4501 Forbes Boulevard, Suite 200, Lanham, Maryland 20706
www.rowman.com

Unit A, Whitacre Mews, 26-34 Stannary Street, London SE11 4AB, United Kingdom

Distributed by NATIONAL BOOK NETWORK

British Library Cataloguing in Publication Information Available

Library of Congress Cataloging-in-Publication Data
Veseth, Mike, 1949–
  Money, taste, and wine : it's complicated! / Mike Veseth.
    pages cm
  Includes bibliographical references and index.
  ISBN 978-1-4422-3463-5 (cloth : alk. paper) — ISBN 978-1-4422-3464-2 (electronic)
1. Wine industry. 2. Viticulture. 3. Wine and wine making. I. Title.
  HD9382.5.V47 2015
  338.4'76632—dc23
                                                                              2015000756

♾™ The paper used in this publication meets the minimum requirements of
American National Standard for Information Sciences—Permanence of Paper for
Printed Library Materials, ANSI/NISO Z39.48-1992.

Printed in the United States of America

Contents

Chapter 1

The Wine Buyer's
Biggest Mistake

The biggest mistake that wine buyers make? Buying books instead of wine. No wait. That can't be right. Let me start again.

Give someone a fish, the old saying goes, and she will eat for a day. Teach her to fish, and she'll eat forever. Good advice, I suppose, but not very useful to me. What about the wine? How am I supposed to enjoy all that fish if I don't have any wine to drink with it?—Sauvignon Blanc if it is Alaskan halibut *beurre blanc*, maybe a nice Pinot Noir if it's grilled Chinook salmon. No end of choices for trout, depending on how it is prepared.

It's just not the same without wine. I won't go so far as to say fish isn't worth eating (or life's not worth living) without a nice glass of red, white, or rosé, but the experience (for me) is greatly diminished. That's the trouble with these wise old sayings—they only give you part of the answer.

THE BIGGEST MISTAKE YOU CAN MAKE

Wine buyers make a lot of mistakes, whether guided by wise old sayings or other sources of advice, which is easy to understand. A typical upscale supermarket in the United States will offer between eight hundred and two thousand unique wine choices. The breadth and depth of choice can be overwhelming. I suppose you could just settle on one wine that satisfies you (searching by trial and error for the most part) and then simply buy that wine again and again and again, the way that I buy Grape Nuts breakfast cereal—but where's the fun in that?

With so many wines to choose from, it is no wonder that wine buyers made hundreds of different mistakes, but the biggest is very easy to say and difficult to overcome: we confuse price with quality and often spend too much on wine. The myth is that more expensive wines are better and that cheaper wines are necessarily inferior. Deep down we know that this is nonsense, because wine is a matter of taste. Are more expensive books always better books? Are more expensive movies, plays, or musical performances always more enjoyable? Does the most expensive menu item at McDonald's make you happier than a good ol' Big Mac? So why do we think wine is different?

One answer is that most of us aren't able to taste all the different wines at various prices, and if we did taste them, we might not trust our own palates to correctly tell good, better, and best. So we make the heroic assumption that if it costs more, it must be better—how else could they charge such a price? And if they have to sell it for less, it must be pretty mediocre stuff. Not everyone thinks this way (reverse wine snobs unite!), but enough do to make a cautious generalization possible.

A typical wine buyer finds a price comfort zone and sticks with it, reaching up to a higher price for special occasions and stooping down to cheaper stuff when quantity is more important than quality. If you were shopping for a wine to bring to a special social function, do you think you would reach up or down? It's instinctive—I catch myself doing it, even though I know better. But it *is* a mistake.

PRICE AND QUALITY BY THE NUMBERS

It isn't very difficult to come up with circumstantial evidence that quality doesn't always rise with price. If you live in the United States, you can probably do all the research you need while you are standing in line to pay at the grocery store. Just choose a long line (so you'll have a little extra time to gather empirical evidence), and then grab a copy of *Wine Spectator, Wine Enthusiast*, or any of the other wine magazines you are likely to find near the checkout stand. Now turn to whatever part of the magazine has the wine ratings (they are in the back in *Wine Spectator*) and take a close look. (Because I insist on playing my own games, I'm going to report from an issue of *Wine Spectator* that was sitting on my desk as I wrote this.[1])

If you page through the wine ratings, you will surely see that some *types* of wines are more expensive than others. But if you drill down *within* a wine category, the notion that higher-priced wines are not necessarily better wines will start to emerge. I'm going to look at the section in this issue on French wines from the Languedoc-Roussillon region.

The top wine in this category is a Côtes du Roussillon-Villages 2009 by the famous winemaker M. Chapoutier. It cost $110 and received a fine score of 92/100. (I'm using *Wine* Spectator's 100-point rating numbers here as a convenient way of making a point, not because such scores are perfect measures of wine quality.) The tasting note makes it sound really yummy—wish I could sample it, but even if I was willing to spend that much money, the chances that I would stumble onto this wine are fairly low—only 150 cases were made, and there are lots of wine drinkers in the world!

Next on the list is another Côtes du Roussillon-Villages wine, this one from the 2011 vintage. Domaine Gardiés made 3,300 cases of it, and while the tasting note is different in detail, the wine sounds just as interesting but costs much less—just $21. The rating? The same 92/100 as the wine by the more famous producer.

Working my way down the list, I find 90-point wines from this region that range from $26 to $57—all different, but all of high quality, according to the *Wine Spectator* tasting panel. My choice? I'd probably look for the 2011 Côtes du Roussillon-Villages Les Vignes de Bila-Haut by that same famous M. Chapoutier. And I might find it, too, since they made forty thousand cases. A very good wine (it earned 88 points) and much more affordable at just $14 a bottle. That's my kind of wine.

Given this, why should you pay more? Maybe there are particular qualities of that first wine that really appeal to you and make it worthwhile for you to spend a bit more to have it. But you don't have to pay more to get quality wine, and you can often get very good wine for much less. You just have to overcome your biggest enemy when it comes to making a good wine decision: yourself.

WHAT MONEY CAN BUY

How much does price matter to our perception of wine? There have been many formal studies that suggest it isn't just about the wine (or just about the money)—context matters a lot.

Robin Goldstein goes to great lengths to remove price from the context when his test subjects sample different wines and he reports the results in his *Wine Trials* book series.[2] He finds that there is basically no correlation between price and the perceived quality, as reported by his human lab rats, for the wines tested. If there is a relationship, it is negative—higher-priced wines score a little lower in the tests, which could be because costlier wines might have more tannins, which some consumers might find less desirable, or that they need longer aging before their special qualities become apparent. In any case, if you can't see the price, you may not be able to taste the difference, which I guess is not surprising given that other studies suggest that wine drinkers are often unable even to tell whether a wine is red or white by taste alone if the color of the wine is hidden from them.

A 2008 study by Antonio Rangel of CalTech and his colleagues took the opposite approach. Rangel told his subjects how much their wine cost, but he didn't always tell the truth. The victims, er, test subjects, would taste the same wine more than once with different price information provided and report their satisfaction. Rangel found that his human guinea pigs generally liked a wine much more when they thought it cost $90 than when the same wine was presented to them as a $10 bottle, and they liked the $45 version of another wine better than when they were told it cost $35.

What made Rangel's study (which was published with the riveting title "Marketing Action Can Modulate Neural Representations of Experienced Pleasantness") more interesting is that he didn't just ask his subjects what they thought, he also scanned their brains using functional magnetic resonance imaging (fMRI) while they were tasting. And as you might guess, just the thought that they were going to taste an expensive wine made parts of the brain that are associated with the experience of pleasure light up on the scans. They didn't just think the wines were better when told they were expensive, they really did enjoy them more.[3]

That's why we are our own worst enemies. We know (or should know) that price doesn't always equal quality, but just tell us that a wine is expensive and our brains get all excited. Are we hardwired to prefer expensive wines? Rangel doesn't think so. He speculates that the brain is simply trying to be efficient and so uses every little bit of information it can to make snap judgments. Once we are conditioned to certain activities or beliefs, we become like

Pavlov's dogs, except we don't salivate at the sound of a bell, we get thirsty at the sight of a price sticker. Who knew?

Reuters wine and money blogger Felix Salmon took Rangel's empirical observations and applied it to the Wall Street crowd he knows so well from writing about finance. His conclusion? Now he knows why so many wealthy people collect fine wine—the more it costs, the happier they are. Let me repeat that, the more it costs, the happier they are—really! Just the thought of how expensive those wines are stimulates their brains and gives them great pleasure.

They say that money can't buy happiness, Salmon concludes. But they're wrong.[4] It can—when you spend it on really, really expensive wine.

RATIONAL EXPECTATIONS

Wine is context-sensitive? I guess that shouldn't come as a surprise, but we sometimes think of taste as something that can be objectively assessed and not influenced by money or other factors. A pair of recent tastings helped me understand just how complicated the taste of wine can be.

A friend asked if I would be willing to speak at a wine tasting that she donated to the local YWCA fund-raising auction. Yes, of course—and I knew at once what I wanted to do: set up a tasting of a flight of red wines made by three fellow University of Puget Sound alumni (Tom Hedges of Hedges Family Estate, Chuck Reininger of Helix and Reininger Cellars, and Michael Corliss of Corliss Estates and Tranche Cellars), but first a blind tasting of white wines that figure prominently in my 2011 book, *Wine Wars*.

If you've read *Wine Wars*, you know that I ended each flight of chapters with a wine tasting designed to explore the themes raised in the book. Three Sauvignon Blancs make up the first flight, and, thus inspired, I put together a tasting of Charles Shaw (a.k.a. Two Buck Chuck) Sauvignon Blanc from California, Robert Mondavi Fumé Blanc from Napa Valley, and Cloudy Bay Marlborough Sauvignon Blanc from New Zealand.

After tasting the three wines blind in the order given above, I asked the tasters to (1) name the grape variety, (2) guess the country or region of origin for each wine, (3) guess the prices, and (4) choose their favorite wine from among the three. I am not a big fan of blind tastings, but this one is fun to do in a group. I thought the auction group would enjoy it (and they did).

But first I decided to try out the blind tasting on my own lab rats, the students who were enrolled in my university course, Idea of Wine, at the time. I was interested to see what the students would do with the blind flight of Sauvignon Blancs. My hypothesis was that students would have more trouble guessing the grape, *terroir,* and price of these wines than would the more experienced wine drinkers in the group that purchased the YWCA auction tasting.

Things did not go according to plan. After tasting the three white wines, the college students were very confused and guessed all the grape varieties they could think of, but not Sauvignon Blanc. For me the signature taste of the Cloudy Bay is a giveaway—Marlborough Sauvignon Blanc—but tasted in the context of the Mondavi Fumé Blanc and Two Buck Chuck wines, which are so very different, nothing seemed to make sense. The common thread that connected the three wines was understandably difficult for these wine novices to detect.

Interestingly, the more experienced tasters in the auction group did no better than the lab rat students in guessing the grape variety. This really did surprise me, and I think it was the confusing context that caused the trouble. Tasting the Mondavi Fumé or the Cloudy Bay by itself might yield a good guess of type of wine or place of origin, but stringing the three wines together apparently distorted the view a bit too much.

One place where there was a significant difference between the groups was in guessing the prices. The experienced auction group did much *worse!* How is that possible? The big difference was the Two Buck Chuck, which generally sells for $3 or less. No frugal college student would offer to pay more than $12 for it after the blind tasting, but at least one member of the auction group was willing to pay $25 or more!

Why were seemingly rational people willing to pay so much for such a modest wine? The quality of the Two Buck Chuck must be part of the answer. Wine drinkers of a certain age (and I include myself in this category) remember when cheap wines were often foul, and then Two Buck Chuck and its bargain-priced siblings changed all that. The wine might not be complex or especially memorable (only a couple of people in the two groups picked it as their favorite of the three), but it does reach a commercial standard that actually shocked and impressed one experienced drinker who had not previously tasted a $2.49 wine.

But the real answer is again probably context. The students were used to me presenting them with wines that are just outside a student's budget—

Part I
BUYER BEWARE!

wines that cost, say, $10 to $30 a bottle. They guessed at the low end of that range, which made sense given their expectations and the fact that the Charles Shaw wine is not very complex. The auction group's higher guess also reflected context. Who would expect to attend a charity auction tasting and be served such a simple, inexpensive wine? Impossible! So it *must* cost a lot, the logic probably went, and "I just can't taste the difference." If true, this is a classic case of using price (or expected price) as a proxy for perceived quality.

In other words, they simply assumed a high price, and, like Rangel's test subjects, their brains began to glow in anticipation. They enjoyed the experience so much they didn't especially notice that the wine wasn't as complex as they might have expected.

Which was the favorite wine? The auction group was pretty much divided between the Mondavi Fumé and Cloudy Bay. The students were divided, too, but Cloudy Bay received most of the votes. That Marlborough style is so distinctive—like nothing they ever had before—and in a blind tasting context it stood out to them.

What conclusion can we draw from these two tastings? Our perception of wine is sometimes less about truth and more about context and expectations than we might want to think. That's not the conclusion I thought I would find when I set up this tiny experiment, but taken in the context of what I've said so far, I probably should have expected it.

ARE PRICE AND QUALITY TOTALLY UNRELATED?

So is the idea that you get more when you pay more totally bogus? Not entirely, but I hope by now I have persuaded you that it is wrong to believe that higher-priced wines are always better. Better ingredients generally cost more in making wine, as with most other things, so looking at it strictly from the supply side of the equation, sometimes you have to spend more to get more.

Take grapes as an example. One ton of wine grapes makes about sixty cases of wine. How much do wine grapes cost? It depends on the variety and grape quality. The average price of one ton of Napa Valley Cabernet Sauvignon grapes was around $4,500 in 2011, according to Allied Grape Growers data. These grapes will be of top quality from low-yielding vines planted on good sites, of course, and their use will also allow you to specify "Napa Valley" on the label, which is an advantage in the market place. Using the "1 percent" rule of thumb for winemaking, you would only pay $4,500 for one ton of grapes if you expected to charge at least $4,500 × 1 percent = $45 per bottle for the wine.

You don't have to pay this much for one ton of Cabernet Sauvignon—grapes from the Paso Robles region sold for an average price of $1,072 in 2011. The same grape variety from the Lodi area sold for $633, and San Joaquin Valley Cab grapes were just $486. This is an amazing range of prices—the Napa grapes on average were nearly ten times the cost of the Central Valley grapes. And these are just averages. Imagine how much the very best Napa grapes must have cost compared to the lowest quality available!

Why such a big cost difference? The physical conditions for growing the grapes are much different in the hot San Joaquin Valley than they are in the Napa Valley, which is closer to the sea. Land costs are higher in Napa, too, but that is because the grape prices are higher, so it is a circular explanation. The cheaper grapes are grown in the San Joaquin Valley on vast, heavily irrigated farms using efficient mechanical pruning and harvesting techniques and conventional (read "we use all the standard and approved sprays and preparations") agricultural methods. Yields can be very high—10 tons per acre and more depending on variety. All factors point to quantity at a standard commercial quality. The grapes are healthy, the wines they make can be good, but growing conditions don't make an attempt to reach for the stars very feasible.

Things are very different in the North Coast regions of Napa and Sonoma. The vineyards will be planted very densely *not* to grow more grapes, but to force the vines to compete with each other so that they make fewer but better grapes (and waste less energy on shoot and leaf growth). Yields will be much lower—2 tons per acre or less depending on the grape variety and vineyard site. Old vines are nurtured here, too, the lower productivity of the vines (some are more than one hundred years old) is offset by the intensity of the taste. Much more of the work will be done by hand, of course, at additional expense, and conventional sprays and treatments are sometimes replaced by organic or biodynamic viticulture.

It is easy to see why the best wine grapes (and therefore, at least potentially, the best wines) are more expensive than the ordinary, but this example only scratches the surface of the factors that can add or subtract cost. Many red wines (and some white ones, too) are aged for a time in oak barrels. Many of the world's "cult wines" are aged in 100 percent, first-use French oak, and this is an expensive process. Each barrel costs $1,000 or more and holds just

30 gallons (25 cases or 300 bottles) of wine, so the oak alone adds about $3.33 to the cost of a bottle of the wine if all of it is aged in new barrels. It is easy to see that your $10 bottle of Chilean Cabernet doesn't cost enough to warrant such lavish investment, but it still probably gets an oak treatment (albeit less expensive), such as partly new and partly second- or third-use oak barrels. Other cost-cutting techniques include inserting new oak staves into used oak barrels or simply hanging bags of oak chips in a tank of wine, a technique favored by "postmodern" winemaker Clark Smith.[5]

THE PRICE IS RIGHT

Do better ingredients and techniques, such as superior grapes and French oak barrels, make better wine than the cheaper alternatives? Yes, they can, but it all depends on the skill of the winemaker in using them. And a technically better wine might not be to your particular taste compared with a lower-priced wine that succeeds in pushing your personal buttons. Fair enough, but doesn't this story seem to suggest that, in some general way, better wine *should* cost more because it uses more expensive ingredients?

No, because while the cost of making a bottle of wine certainly influences its price, it doesn't determine it. In most cases, the price of wine is based on what consumers are willing to pay as much as the cost of making it. It certainly costs more to make a bottle of a Napa Valley cult wine like Screaming Eagle (or a first-growth Bordeaux, like Château Mouton Rothschild) than it does higher production wine, such as Beringer Knights Valley Cabernet, Columbia Crest Grand Estates Cabernet, or Mouton Cadet Rouge, a mass-produced Bordeaux blend, but the difference in cost is far less than the difference in price (more than $500 a bottle for the Screaming Eagle, for example, and less than $25 for the Beringer Cab, or less than half that amount for the Columbia Crest or Mouton Cadet).

Expensive wines have higher prices, both when they are very good and when they are less so, because buyers are willing to pay those prices. Less-expensive wines may be better, worse, or equally good as their more expensive shelf-mates depending upon how the market perceives them. Your trick, as a wine buyer, is much the same as a financial investor—to find something that pleases you but is undervalued in the market so that you can enjoy both the wine and the savings!

THE GREAT MISTAKE: A RANT

Now it's time for my first rant (I'm issuing this warning just in case rants and raves aren't to your taste). It is bad enough that our brains work against us when we are trying to avoid the biggest mistake that wine drinkers can make, but I guess we are just hardwired that way, and we have only ourselves to blame.

But (and here's the rant part), do wine producers and retailers have to exploit our weaknesses so ruthlessly? OK, I suppose they do (wine is a business, after all, and it is sometimes necessary to exploit the weaknesses of others), but it still bugs me. You may have observed many retailers organizing wine according to place of origin (California, France, etc.) and, in the New World sections by grape variety (Chardonnay, Pinot Noir, etc.). But have you noticed that there is often a third type of placement according to price? The most expensive wines are frequently on the higher shelves and the cheaper stuff down near the floor. This encourages us to think that higher (in both price and product placement) is better and that lower is, well, lower.

In fact, the variation in quality *within* a given price range may be greater in some cases than the differences *between* wines that sell at different prices. But that price-based stratification erases everything that you might have learned and replaces it with a clear image: if you want to go to the heights of pleasure, you just pull out your credit card and make your way to the top of the wine wall where the most expensive bottles reside.[6]

Wineries sometimes play this game, too, raising the price rather than lowering it to try to establish reputation and encourage sales. One of the most successful practitioners of this strategy, at least according to some, is Angelo Gaja, who is often credited with raising the profile of wines from the Piedmont region of Italy. Gaja's tricks? Investments in the vineyard and the use of expensive new oak barrels—real winemaking techniques—plus that audacity to set a very high price. If Gaja can charge such astronomic sums, the logic goes, his wines must be spectacular.[7] They are, of course, but they might not have gotten so much attention so quickly without Gaja's bold pricing strategy. I am pretty sure that some wineries use high price as a signal of quality whether the quality is there or not.

So what are we to do? When it comes to buying wine, our brains betray us, and the sellers understand and aren't afraid to exploit our weakness. Self-awareness is key (as I will explain in Chapter 3), but knowledge is power, too, because the relationship among money, taste, and wine is complicated.

Chapter 2

Anatomy of a
Complicated Relationship

Some say that wine is the world's most sensuous beverage, which is why people love it so. It stimulates all the physical senses—taste, touch, see, smell, and even "hear" if you touch glasses before drinking (cheers!), as wine drinkers are wont to do. *Most* sensuous? That's hard to prove, but wine's sensuous nature is a good reason to embrace it.

But the taste of wine isn't the only thing that influences our experience of it, as we have just seen. The wine buyer's biggest mistake is to confuse the sense of wine with the dollars and cents of it. Money, taste, and wine are so tightly linked that sometimes it seems like it's impossible to pry them apart. Maybe we should look more closely at the ties that bind them together and what they have to say about our ever-expanding world of wine.

Don't expect this to be a linear journey—my three muses are hard to control. Taste and wine are intricately intertwined, but taste has many meanings and takes many forms in wine, as in other areas of life. There is what you actually taste when you taste wine—the sensory element—and then there is the subjective standard of taste—the idea that someone might have good taste in wine or bad taste in wine. Wine critics who write for magazines or judge wine competitions are often thought to set an objective standard of taste—to know what a particular wine *should* taste like. Famous wine critics like Robert Parker are known for their taste and sometimes criticized for the power that their taste commands in the marketplace and the incentive that winemakers face to make wines in particular ways to please them. Why would someone make a "Parkerized" wine (one calculated to appeal to a famous critic's palate)? For the glory of a 100-point score, I suppose, but mainly for the profit that a high rating is likely to produce.

Which brings us inevitably to money. It is difficult these days to have a serious discussion about anything—food, art, music, sport, politics—without money coming up at some point. Although we may dream of a world where wine flows free, the reality of money cannot be ignored. Indeed, as we shall see, when it comes to wine, money affects every imaginable definition of taste. And so money is the third dancer in this book's eponymous *ménage à trois*.[1] Money, taste, and wine are certainly linked—is this a good thing? What sort of "relationship" do they have?

When I first set up my account on Facebook, I had to choose a "relationship status." Married? Single? Engaged? There were several conventional options, and then one that really caught my eye: "It's Complicated." Yes, I think we have all been there at some point in our business, social, or family lives. "It's complicated" is the short description of a type of relationship that seems to defy short descriptions. You can't reduce it to one quick word or phrase like "divorced" or "going steady."

One of the most complicated types of relationships is a triangle. A loves B, who is really more interested in C, who doesn't care for B at all but has a secret crush on A. Can they all live happily ever after? All's well that ends well, I suppose, but not every complicated relationship has an ending as satisfying as a Shakespeare play. I'm no playwright, but I could write a book about the complicated relationship between and among money, taste, and wine. In fact, I have—and you are holding it in your hands now.

THE WINE LOVER'S TRILEMMA

I seem to specialize in complicated relationships. Not in my personal life ("happily married" is my long-standing status) but in my professional work. As a university professor my particular specialty is the study of globalization and all the complicated and interwoven patterns it creates. Then there's the other side of my professional life, my career as a wine economist where I study the global wine markets and write about them on my blog, *The Wine*

Economist (WineEconomist.com) and in books like *Wine Wars* and *Extreme Wine*. That's how I got interested in this money, taste, and wine combination.

It would be great if this were a simple love triangle: taste loves wine, wine needs money, money enables taste, or something like that, but I think it's more complicated than that. I fear, in fact, that it might be a *trilemma*, one of the particular types of complicated relationships that I write about frequently when I'm wearing my global economist's hat. What's a trilemma? Basically it is like a dilemma, but more complicated. What a surprise! A dilemma presents you with a choice—should I stay or should I go? Not always an easy decision to make. A trilemma adds a further twist, making the decision even more difficult and the relationship more complex. Maybe an example is the best way to begin.

Welcome to the lunch-hour trilemma, where you can't always get what you want. When I go out for lunch in the middle of a busy workday, there are usually three things I look for. The food should be good—because life is too short to eat bad food (or drink bad wine)—it should be fast, since I need to get back to work, and it should be cheap, or at least not needlessly costly. Good, fast, and cheap—these are my typical lunchtime desires, and a lot of the time I can have them all, which is great. But I have noticed that when the dining situation is pushed to the extreme (because of sudden surge of customers, for example, or if I'm really in a rush), the good–fast–cheap lovefest breaks down, and I am left with a trilemma choice. Pick any two—good or fast or cheap—but forget getting all three. Here's how it works.

I can get good and fast, but it might not be cheap. If it was cheap, then everyone would be eating it, and it wouldn't be fast any more, or maybe the quality would suffer. Or I can get fast and cheap, but it might not be very good (if it was good, everyone would want to eat it and so they'd have to raise the prices). Or I can get cheap and good, but I will have to wait a long, long time for a table! Do you see the trilemma effect? Pick any two of the three—good, fast, and cheap—and under stressful conditions you will have to give up the remaining quality. Good, fast, cheap—choose any two! It's enough to make you stay home and prepare your own lunch, except that the trilemma sometimes applies there, too.

The idea of a trilemma didn't originate at a shopping mall food court, it was actually invented to describe certain problems in international finance.[2]

But trilemmas can appear anywhere there is a complicated relationship—an *Economist* magazine columnist recently diagnosed a health-care trilemma that you might recognize. "Health systems have to choose among the 'three Cs'—cost, coverage and choice," according to "Buttonwood," who writes about economic policy. "A country can have universal health coverage, as in the British system, but at the expense of choice. Or it can have lots of patient choice, as in America, but only by limiting coverage or allowing costs to escalate (or both)."[3] Trilemmas at lunch. Trilemmas in global finance. Trilemmas at the doctor's office. Trilemmas in wine, too? Perhaps!

Money, taste, and wine: you want them all, and you can have them all when conditions are right. But sometimes, maybe when it matters most, you might have to choose. Pick two and be prepared to sacrifice the third. That's what a wine trilemma would look like. Is this how money, taste, and wine work? Let's work through the logic of the situation one side of the triangle at a time and see what we think.

WINE + MONEY = NO TASTE

Add money to wine and taste is destroyed. Can this be true? This trilemma proposition was the theme of Jonathan Nossiter's classic 2004 film, *Mondovino*.[4] The heroes of this film are winemakers who are committed to tradition, to authenticity, to taste, and, because of that, I suppose, they struggle to survive, their very existence is constantly threatened. By what? By whom? Why, by money, of course, and the winery corporations who have sold out to the gods of global commerce. Taste has been replaced by media hype, since the moneymen and winemakers are obviously in bed with the tasteless critics, or at least that's what some of the characters in *Mondovino* seem to suggest.

I am a critic of Nossiter's critique because I think that the relationship with money is more complicated than his characters indicate, but I admit that his equation does sometimes hold. Money is very useful to a winemaker, but sometimes adding money to wine is like pouring gasoline on a raging fire. A great example is Inglenook wine, which was in the 1930s possibly the best but surely one of the most expensive wines of California. Taste was what gave Inglenook its initial place in history, but it was money that drove its sale during

World War II to a profit-hungry drinks corporation. Wartime price controls made it impossible to raise wine prices—unless you found a way to sell your drinks under a brand that was already pricey. Suddenly, Inglenook was worth more for its potential to get around the price-control laws than for the actual wines themselves. Inglenook tumbled from premium product to overpriced plonk. Ouch! The brand changed hands several times after the war, its former life as a wine of taste nearly forgotten, before it was finally rescued by film director and winery mogul Francis Ford Coppola, who now seeks to restore Inglenook's taste and place in history.

Is Inglenook's sad tale (with a happy ending) a special case or part of the general pattern that *Mondovino* explored? You must be the judge of that. In any case, it illustrates the first side of the trilemma.

WINE + TASTE = NO MONEY

It has long been known that the easiest way to make a small fortune in the wine business is to start with a large one, so the second trilemma choice is not really news. Wine lovers write to me frequently for advice about buying a vineyard or opening a winery, and I always cringe just a bit when they talk about their passion for wine. Passion is great—I certainly love what I do and I wish others the same satisfaction—but passion (which you may think of for this purpose as a variation on taste) is sometimes the enemy when it comes to making good business decisions, which is why it is good to begin a winemaking venture with lots of ready cash.

I was reminded of this side of the struggle among money, taste, and wine by a pair of recent books by Caro Feely, *Grape Expectations* (2012) and *Saving Our Skins* (2014).[5] Caro and her husband, Sean, and their two young daughters moved from Dublin, Ireland, to France, following their dream to make a living making the sort of fine wines that they are passionate about. They quit their jobs, sold their home, uprooted the family, and purchased a vineyard and winery in Saussignac, an appellation adjacent to Bordeaux, and began the difficult work. Caro's books could easily have turned their tale into a romantic saga in the mode of *A Year in Provence* or *Under the Tuscan Sun*, but they didn't. Instead, three stories are deftly interwoven—the personal story of the Feelys and their friends and neighbors, the technical story of how grapes are grown and wine is made, and the business story of what a struggle it is to hold onto the small fortune that they invested in their venture and not see the whole enterprise go down the drain. You won't be surprised to learn that it is the economic story that most appeals to me. It is a perfect illustration of a situation that plagues thousands of winemakers around the world.

Is it *possible* to make great wine and money, too? Of course, so the trilemma trade-off doesn't always hold. But trilemmas aren't about what happens in good times but about what has to happen when things go wrong, as they so often do, in the vineyard or in the cellar, and that's when wine plus taste becomes the enemy of profit.

TASTE + MONEY = NO WINE

OK, now it gets tricky. The third leg of the wine lover's trilemma is logically the notion that the combination of money and taste are inconsistent with wine, at least when pushed to the extreme. *Sacré bleu*—that's sacrilege! It seems pretty obvious that money and taste go naturally with wine. In fact, it seems like a perfect pairing (or triplet or whatever you get when three things go together very well). How can I possibly justify this final piece of the trilemma puzzle? I am not really sure . . . maybe I can't! But I can at least draw upon an authority in my defense.

The people of Paris must have lots of money—how else could they afford to live in one of the most expensive cities in Europe or maybe the world? And they must have taste, too, since Paris is the home to so much great art, architecture, music, fashion, and food. So they must love wine, too, right? Especially since they are French and everyone knows that wine is the French national drink. But incredibly this seems not to be so, at least according to one expert. Money and taste, yes. But no wine!

My authority is Oliver Mangy, author of the 2011 book *Stuff Parisians Like.*[6] Parisians apparently like lots of stuff, which makes sense because of their abundant money and taste endowments. Parisians like conversation, for example, but it is not about *having* an exchange of ideas, according to Mangy, it is about *winning* the exchange. Conversation, to a Parisian, is a contest, and there is always a winner and a loser. This explains a lot about my Parisian friend, who will never give up on a losing side of a conversation. Choosing at random from the short, punchy list of chapter topics, Parisians apparently like the following:

- Having Theories (like my trilemma?)
- Making Lists (like this one)
- Crossing the Street in a Bold Way
- Saying They Like Classical Music
- Bitching about Waiters
- The Idea of Moving Overseas
- The Idea of Sailing
- New York
- Urinating in the Street
- UNICEF Cards
- Bashing Tourists
- Scarves and Wearing Black
- Despising *les PSG* (you need to be a soccer fan to understand this one)

And so on for more than 250 pages.

I admit that I enjoyed this tour of the Parisian psyche, but I soon became impatient. What about wine? What kind of wine "stuff" do Parisians, with all their money and taste, really like? I expected to read about wine right at the start, but, by about page 200, I began to worry that wine might never appear. I was almost right. Wine was invisible until page 274 (right after the chapter on why Parisians like Barack Obama). The last chapter is titled (why Parisians like . . .) "Not Drinking Wine."

Zut Alors! (I learned that in my seventh-grade French class—Magny teaches that a Parisian would probably say, "*Putain!*" instead.) "It is very easy to spot tourists in a Parisian cafe," Magny writes, "They are the ones drinking wine." Having a glass of wine gives the tourists pleasure. *Not drinking wine* is what Parisians like to do. Magny operates a wine bar and wine school in Paris, so it is with obvious frustration that he enumerates all the reasons wine has fallen from grace in Paris. Once it was the default choice, he says, but now young people especially understand that they have many choices, most of which are easier to comprehend and have better marketing behind them. Water, beer, and spirits—these are the go-to beverages of Paris now. Money gives you the ability to choose, and taste trumps tradition, so wine is left out.

Women are a particular problem, Mangy says. They think drinking wine makes them fat and encourages them to lose control. No Parisian woman would want that! When Parisians do drink wine, he says, they drink bad wine. This is especially true for the *bobos* (bourgeois bohemians) who flock to wine bars specializing in *vins naturels* ("natural wines," made with minimum manipulation), which hide their obvious technical flaws under a cloak of "authenticity," he suggests. I guess this is evidence that Parisians like "Having a Theory" (real wine = natural wine) more than they like actually "Not Drinking Wine." Parisians are complicated people!

A GENERAL THEORY OF COMPLICATION?

So does Paris prove that the wine lover's trilemma holds? No, I suppose not. I think it strengthens my case, that's for sure, but I admit it isn't hard proof. I introduced the trilemma in order to suggest that the triangle formed by money, taste, and wine is a complicated one, and I think I have demonstrated that point pretty well. But does the trilemma really *explain* the situation? No! Of course not! The way that money, taste, and wine are intertwined is much more complicated than a simple trilemma. And so I have had to write this book to break the relationship down and then put it back together. I invite you to come along for the journey.

We begin with a trio of chapters that I file under the general category "Buyer Beware!" Beware of the tendency to confuse price and quality. Beware of the temptation to think that money, taste, and wine are simple things. And, as you will see in the next chapter, beware of the idea that everyone is the same when it comes to the taste of wine. "Wine Drinker, Know Thyself" is the title of Chapter 3, and I'll give you some useful tips on how to take your knowledge of wine and knowledge of yourself to the next level.

"Get a Clue! Searching for Buried Treasures" is the title of Part II. We will explore dump bucket wines, Treasure Island wines, really big-box wines, looking for the perfect money–taste–wine balance. And we will discover that sometimes the best wine is really a beer. Oh my!

If a rose is a rose is a rose as Shakespeare has it, is a rosé just a rosé? Not once it is branded and has a clever label to give it an identity. In Part III, we'll explore how labels influence us and the relationship between wine identity and our identity, finishing with the wine with the strongest identity of all— Champagne.

Finally, in Part IV, we examine "What Money Can (and Can't) Buy," considered first in restaurants, then as investment wines, and on to wines that no amount of money can buy. Can wine do more than satisfy our thirst—can it change the world one cork at a time? Perhaps, as we shall learn in the final chapter, where I'll tell you about my groot (great) expectations and then take you on a truck ride deep into the bush, to gaze into the starry sky and ponder what money, taste, and wine can tell us about life

Life? Life? That's complicated, too, don't you think, with money and taste in constantly shifting configurations. No wonder wine is the best way to understand it. *Salut!*

Chapter 3

Wine Drinker,
Know Thyself!

Making a decision can be a nightmare when there are too many options. Maybe that's why some travelers opt for the "tourist menu" when they are in a foreign country (or seek out the nearest McDonald's for a Big Mac attack). The food may or may not always be a good value or especially distinctive cuisine, but the set menu represents blessed simplicity in a sea of unfamiliar choices.

Economists call this the "Paradox of Choice," and I am sure that we have all experienced that overwhelmed feeling that comes when we are forced to confront an unexpected range of choices. There isn't a special version of the Paradox of Choice for wine, but I suppose there could be since wine comes in so many varieties, styles, and price ranges. Sometimes it is enough to make you long for the simple choice—"A bottle of red, a bottle of white"?—of the old Billy Joel song "Scenes from an Italian Restaurant." One Washington State winery has prospered by offering wines under the "House" brand, as in "House Red" and "House White." Can't get much simpler than that! You could adopt the strategy of simplify, simplify, simplify and do very well, I suppose, but chances are that you wouldn't be reading this book if you weren't a bit adventurous. So what's the alternative?

The conventional wisdom is that knowledge is power when it comes to wine as in so many other things, so the obvious solution is to learn as much as you can about the wine choices available to you. I think this is great advice, and I encourage you to develop a geeky interest in wine. Try lots of different wines and make notes of the ones you like and the ones you don't. Don't have pen and paper to write down the name of that wine you had at your friends' house? What do you think that camera in your mobile phone is for? Photograph the label and look it up on the Web when you get home.

While I am all in favor of trying to learn everything there is to know about wine, I admit that it is an endless quest. There are so many wines already, and new wineries and new wines appear each week. You can equip yourself with research materials like wine atlases and guides—there is even a best-selling book called *The Wine Bible*.[1] (Hmmm, I wonder if it has a chapter called Genesis that begins, "In the beginning there was wine, and God saw the wine and said it was good.") My favorite reference books are *The Oxford Companion to Wine*,[2] an endlessly fascinating encyclopedia of wine edited by Jancis Robinson, and the massively detailed *Wine Grapes*, by Jancis Robinson, Julia Harding, and José Vouillamoz,[3] which tells all about 1,368 different grapes and the wines they can make. Wine geek paradise!

All these guides and references are useful, but there's something that you need to find out before all this information can do you any good. What kind of a wine drinker are you—really?

THE KNOW THYSELF STRATEGY

There are three elements to the "know thyself" strategy: hardware, software, and, of course, money. All men (and women) are created equal according to the law here in the United States, but the rule fails when it comes to our ability to taste wine. Everyone has different "hardware"—the physical ability to sense aromas and flavors—and this is one important reason why a wine that your friend might rave about will fail to move your pleasure needle even a notch. *De gustibus non est disputandum* ("you cannot argue about matters of taste") is the unofficial motto of the economics profession, and it probably should be printed on every wine label, too.

Sense of smell is the most important bit of a wine drinker's hardware. Try tasting wine when you have a stuffy nose (or put a clothespin over your nose) and you will understand how much wine appreciation depends upon a good sense of smell.[4] The nose contains hundreds of complex and varied receptors that can detect about a thousand different distinct aromas. People differ in their ability to sense specific odors, how that odor is perceived, and how it is described. The compound androsterone, for example, has a sweet smell to some but a urine aroma to others. Anyone who has taken part in a wine-tasting group knows that the ability to perceive and describe aromas can be improved through practice. And University of California professor Ann Noble's Wine Aroma Wheel[5] has helped many wine enthusiasts get more from each sniff by providing a friendly analytical framework. But the source of the differences between and among wine drinkers is hardware (genes) not just software (wine knowledge and learned abilities).

There are only five basic components to taste: bitter, sweet, salt, sour, and the savory taste of umami. Genetic variations mean that we differ in our ability to sense each one—the range of responses to bitterness is especially great. The difference of a single gene can be responsible for a significant variation in perception of a given bitter compound. A single gene! That's sensitive hardware.

Differences in wine-tasting hardware mean that about 20 percent of the population are "supertasters" who are hardwired to be have an exaggerated reaction to bitterness, and another 20 percent are bitter-tolerant "nontasters," who have a much diminished reaction. The rest of us are "tasters" in this taxonomy, endowed with varying abilities to perceive the chemical compounds in our wine glass. You can check out your own hardware by counting your taste buds. Cut a one-centimeter-square hole in a note card, put a little blue food coloring in your mouth, go up to a mirror, stick out your tongue, and look at it through the hole. Welcome to the supertaster club if you count about 150 bright-blue taste buds in that little square. A nontaster has about fifty taste buds per square centimeter, and average tasters are in the middle, with about one hundred. Scientists understand that supertasters are different, but it's not entirely clear why. Why does having more taste buds mainly increase sensitivity to bitterness as opposed to increasing all flavors? Why do supertasters react so much to red wine even when there are no special bitter compounds? The hardware is obviously complicated, and many questions remain.

Is it good to be a supertaster? Not necessarily. The exaggerated ability to sense bitterness makes supertasters different, that's all. Don't be a snob and look down on a friend who drinks caramel vanilla lattes and loves to slurp down glasses of Moscato or White Zinfandel. She (because there is a bias toward females) may simply be a supertaster.

One thing seems clear: if you have different hardware than your friend (or a famous critic), you will certainly have a different experience of a particular wine. There are no right answers when it comes to wine tasting. Everyone really is different, and what should matter most to you is what you taste and enjoy.

FROM BUDOMETER TO VINOTYPE

When writing about these types of tasters, I was struck by a distant memory of . . . the Budometer! I recalled reading an article in the *Wall Street Journal* some years ago about a wine expert who had taken the qualitative differences in personal wine perception and pushed them to the next level by quantifying them through painstaking experimentation. The result was the Budometer, which was not a measurement of how many Budweisers a person could drink (that would be interesting, too), but a way to determine what types of wines an individual consumer might prefer, with the seemingly inevitable trial-and-error phase eliminated. Budometer, as in taste *buds*, like the ones you counted on your blue tongue a few paragraphs ago.

It seemed like a great idea when I read about it, but I admit that I didn't do much with it at the time. But it was easy enough to find that old *WSJ* interview online, and so I set about to retrace my steps.

I have bad news to report. The Budometer is no more. It seems that some obscure brewing company's lawyers were concerned about the name. But don't despair because it's been replaced by something new, the Vino-type. And the wine expert who got all this started is still at it, too. His name is Tim Hanni, and he's a famous person in American wine. He and Joel Butler were the first Americans to pass the devilishly difficult Master of Wine exam. Fewer than four hundred people in the world have successfully navigated the rigorous process that gives them the right to wear the initials "MW" next to their names.

I've never met Hanni, but he seems like an unusually interesting person. He's had a fabulous career in the wine and hospitality industry (he's also a gourmet chef), and although he knows pretty much all there is to know about wine, he doesn't drink the stuff (or any alcohol) any more. His mission now is to help others enjoy the beverage that he no longer imbibes.

Hanni's research indicates that wine drinkers are hardwired into four basic groups, or Vinotypes, which he calls Sweet, Hypersensitive, Sensitive, and Tolerant. It you want to know all about Hanni's system, you should probably read his 2013 book, *Why You Like the Wines You Like,*[6] or visit his websites: www.timhanni.com and www.myVinotype.com. I'll provide a quick summary here, but you should seek out the more complete reports.

"Sweet" wine tasters are very sensitive to anything that assaults their senses (not just in wine, according to Hanni). Bitterness and alcohol in wine must be covered up with a blanket of sweetness. Women (about one in five) are three times more likely to be Sweet Vinotypes. White Zinfandel is their kind of wine. It isn't a lack of sophistication (White Zin drinkers get a bad rap in wine circles), it's just the way they are built.

A little more than a third of both men and women in Hanni's surveys are "Hypersensitive" Vinotypes. They have intense sensory experiences, as the name suggests. Hanni says they love fragrances and "revel" in aromatic memories. Rather than cover up offending flavors with sweetness, however, they instead seek out delicate wines that are dry or off-dry, aromatic (obviously), and very smooth. They avoid big red wines with lots of oak (or any wine with overt oak treatment). Sparkling wines, drier Rieslings, and Sauvignon Blancs fit this profile very well, along with lighter reds, like Pinot Noir.

"Sensitive" Vinotypes make up about a quarter of the wine-drinking population, and Hanni says they are the most adventurous drinkers (and eaters, too). They like to try new things. Accordingly, they enjoy a broad range of red and white wines and lean towards the drier side of the sweetness spectrum.

"Tolerant" Vinotypes are less sensitive when it comes to harsh, bitter sensations such as you might find in rugged, high-alcohol red wines. Given a choice, Hanni says, Tolerant Vinotypes head for the reds like Cabernet Sauvignon and are not daunted by high alcohol levels, because the smack of the alcohol is mitigated by a deceptive sweetness that they perceive even in a completely dry wine. You won't be surprised to learn that men outnumber women two to one among Tolerant Vinotypes. The next time you see a couple drinking in opposite directions—he with a big, bold Aussie Shiraz and she sipping a delicate Oregon Pinot Gris, don't shake your head, just appreciate that you've stumbled onto a "mixed marriage," Tolerant male and Sensitive female.

YOU ARE WHAT YOU DRINK

The key to the Hanni's Vinotype analysis is the observation that people are very different from each other and that their wine preferences are not just about wine—they reflect a person's sensibilities more generally. Thus, in one incident reported in his book, Hanni pressed an apparently Hypersensitive Vinotype all the way and asked if, by chance, he sometimes wore his underwear inside out (to avoid the relative harshness of the interior seams). "How did you know!" came the very startled response. But it wasn't the underpants story that made Hanni's research memorable for me, it was the original Budometer questionnaire, because Hanni sought to discover wine preferences by asking about other things. How do you like your coffee? Not at all? Straight black? Cream? Sugar and cream? How many sugars? Coffee is pretty bitter, and so I suspect you can already see where this clever question will lead. Hate coffee? Maybe you are Hypersensitive. Like it with cream and two or three sugars? Sweet, I suspect. Straight black? Hello, Mr. Tolerant. I remember having lunch with a group of winemakers in Cape Town, South Africa, a few years ago and noticed that I was the only one taking my coffee black. My relative insensitivity to the bitter taste stood out in a group of winemakers where sensitivity to flavors and aromas was a distinct advantage. Other Budometer questions asked about diet drinks and so forth.

When I went to www.myVinotype.com to take the test that's offered there, I found that Hanni has made a lot of progress compared with my coffee and cream memories. The current questionnaire asks about likes and dislikes regarding coffee and tea, salt, diet drinks, and other things. But it also surveyed my attitudes in general a bit to see if I was set in my ways or more open to new experiences. It even wondered if I liked soft towels, which I recognized as a question that Hypersensitives and Tolerants would answer differently. At the end of the short survey the answer was revealed: I am Sensitive (but not Hypersensitive). Apparently, my ability to tolerate black coffee is offset by my interest in new experiences generally and new wine experiences in particular (an occupational advantage for someone who writes about global wine). The coffee question stuck in my mind, but there is much more to Vinotypes than Starbucks.

And here's why I predict that you will log onto Hanni's website as soon as you can. The Vinotype analysis included a list of about a dozen specific wines that others who are hardwired the way I am have enjoyed. The list included a few wines that I know and love and a number of others that I cannot wait to try (I guess it is that Sensitive thing!). Just to be evil, I played the game again, but this time provided completely false answers regarding my tastes and preferences. You are Hypersensitive, the webpage advised (so at least I know what I am not) and then gave an explanation and another list of wine recommendations. Looking at the list, I was struck by the fact that I love some of those wines, too (especially the Pinot Noirs). I guess this confirms that I am broad-mindedly Sensitive after all.

WHAT THE VINOTYPES TELL US

I hope you take Hanni's test and find out your Vinotype. It's fun and also useful to think seriously about your habits, attitudes, and sensory experiences. What will you learn when you are finished? Apart from Hanni's cool list of suggested wines, I hope this helps you accept that people really are different when it comes to wine—and other things in life. There is no reason why you should like everything your friends like in wine (and indeed there are good reasons why you might disagree). If you are a Sweet Vinotype, you are never going to enjoy that Napa Cabernet, and the Cab lover is never going to understand your passion for Moscato D'Asti. But this doesn't mean that there is no common ground at all. Hanni's analysis shows that there are some wines that span the Vinotypes and can be enjoyed by (almost) all—Pinot Noir, for example, and Zinfandels that are not over the top on the alcohol scale, which are admittedly getting hard to find.

Hanni has gone far beyond the Vinotype in his research, and I encourage you to check out his work because there is a lot that might stimulate your imagination (if you are a Sensitive type) or challenge your firmly held habits and beliefs (if you are on the Sweet side and unwilling to break out of your comfortable routine). One of the more controversial lines of enquiry regards matching of food and wine (remember that Hanni is both a Master of Wine and a masterful chef). He argues that the notion that there are perfect wine and food pairings is as bogus as the idea that there are right answers about wine (you can imagine what he has to say about wine critics and their ratings). When it comes to pairing food and wine, he suggests, eat what you like and drink what you like and they will mainly match very well (because, of course, they are both affected by your same sensory preferences), and, if they don't match up, so what? Match the wine to the diner not the dinner, he says. You are more likely to enjoy yourself if you simply follow your tastes than by following rules that lead you into the opposite direction of your Vinotype.

The flip side of this is that Hanni argues that most foods can be made to taste good with most wines (he writes about an unexpected red wine and oyster combination, for example). The key is to balance the food, often using lemon juice and salt. I haven't explored this idea yet, but it seems like a good excuse to play with my food (and wine), which is something I have always enjoyed.

Know thyself (and thy Vinotype) and honor thy palate while respecting others with different sensory perceptions. I think you will save a lot of money on trial-and-error wine purchases if you accept that you might never like that Cab, on the one hand, or always prefer it, on the other. Experiment and don't get into a rut, but don't assume that you are wrong about what you like just because you are different.

FOLLOW THE MONEY

If know thyself is good advice when it comes to tasting and enjoying wine, it is even better counsel when it comes to paying for the stuff. Some people think nothing of laying down a pile of bills to purchase a bottle of wine, but others hesitate to buy even the cheapest bottles. Why?

The easy answer is that some people have more income or wealth than others, so they can "afford" to spend more money on wine. But there are quotes around "afford" here because ability to pay and willingness to pay are two different things. I know some wealthy people who won't pay more than $10 for a bottle of wine (and some who balk at $5) and others who have less income but happily spend more. Affordability is related to the concept that economists call "opportunity cost." How do you feel about buying wine in this standard textbook economics way of looking at things depends upon how much you enjoy it compared with the alternative opportunities you are giving up. Someone who really enjoys a certain wine may be willing to sacrifice a lot of other things to drink it, but another person (perhaps a Sweet Vinotype faced with a tannic Bordeaux wine) would look at the choice and choose almost anything else than that wine.

Textbook economics is a useful framework for understanding how you choose products generally, but we need to understand that wine presents some distinctive features that, though not truly unique, make it something special from an economics standpoint. The first is that although wine itself is fairly clear and easy to see through, the purchase of wine is hardly a transparent transaction. Wine is an "experience good" with a certain level of "buyer beware" risk built in. It is difficult to know if you will enjoy a new wine until you try it, and, of course, by then the money has already been spent. This is why winemakers seek out opportunities to have potential buyers taste their wines at winery tasting rooms, retail outlets, charity events, and wine festivals. Even a small taste can reduce the perceived risk and ease a buyer's anxiety. Here in the United States, the Olive Garden chain of Italian eateries became number one in restaurant wine sales by giving away thousands of bottles of wine in small samples. One taste makes a sale in many cases.

I have observed that, faced with a risky wine-buying decision, many consumers gravitate towards a certain price comfort zone, which represents the risk that they are willing to take in buying a relatively unknown wine. Some of my friends are very risk-averse—they stick to the $5 to $7 price range, or even less. They buy high-volume wines made to a commercial standard that, though not high in an artistic sense, are at least extremely reliable. Day in, day out, year after year, these wines provide a low-risk (if, for some, low-return) bet. Other friends are willing to risk a bit more in the hopes of hitting an occasional jackpot. For years, a friend refused to try a wine priced outside of his $8 comfort zone because he was afraid that he would be able to taste the difference and his lifelong wine-drinking patterns would be upset (he finally did, he could, and they were!). One part of knowing thyself is therefore to accept that you might have a wine comfort zone, too, and to learn to make the best possible choices within it.

Risk is one factor that affects your willingness to pay for wine, and some people are more risk-averse than others. Your attitude towards luxury goods and expensive things in general is another. Some people are simply drawn to luxury goods (even small ones) for the elevated sense that they bring. The products make them feel nice, but the thought of the product's luxury or cost makes them feel even better. This, I suppose, is why people who may not be able to tell the difference in taste are willing to spend much more for Champagne from France than they would for sparkling wine from another place, even if it is, in fact, made by the same French producer.

The opposite side of this coin is inhabited by wine drinkers who can't imagine paying more for a luxury product. They get their kicks from paying less, in a sort of reverse-snob way. The cheaper something is, the better they like it. Sometimes, I fear, they enjoy the thrill of scoring a wine bargain even more than they enjoy the wine itself. Satisfaction comes from spending less (or getting something for free), even if they could afford to pay more and might even find a more expensive wine objectively more pleasing.

The know thyself theory says that you need to understand what gives you comfort and pleasure and to work with that, at least for now, so that wine is something that you enjoy—from both the sensory and economic standpoints—and not something that makes you anxious or annoyed. When it comes to money, taste, and wine, each of us is a special case. If you know what you like and you can resist the temptation to confuse price with pleasure, you are far more likely to be a smart and happy wine drinker.

Part II

GET A CLUE!
SEARCHING FOR
BURIED TREASURES

Chapter 4

Dump Bucket Wines

One of the most memorable moments in the very memorable 2004 Alexander Payne film *Sideways* is the dump bucket scene.[1] Wine snob Miles (played perfectly by Paul Giamatti) uncharacteristically goes to a winery tasting room bar to drink, not to taste. He's just received the bad news that his novel won't be published, and he wants to get drunk. Another taste! Another! He shoves his empty glass toward the poor tasting room server again and again.

Finally the server refuses—enough!—an act that literally drives Miles to drink. He lifts the dump bucket full of spat wine and poured-out drinks and pours it down his throat and over his clothes. How gross! What a powerful statement of how low Miles's self-esteem had plunged. And funny, too. So funny (and powerful and gross) that it appeared again in a 2009 Japanese remake of *Sideways* called *Saidoweizu*[2] and was reprised in a novel called *Vertical*, written by Rex Pickett, whose earlier book, *Sideways*, was the basis for Payne's film.[3]

Having just returned from a big wine festival where the dump buckets weren't emptied often enough so that the gross part of this story is fresh in my mind, let me assure you of one thing. When I talk about the "dump bucket" wines that you might want to check out, I do not mean it literally. Under no circumstances should you lift up that big bucket and take a deep draught! Ugh!

DUMPING WINE . . . AND OTHER THINGS

Dumping has one meaning in the wine world and quite a different meaning in international economics, which I taught for many years at the University of Puget Sound. In international trade, dumping, selling a product for less in a foreign market than at home, is the solution to a particularly annoying problem. Suppose that you have spent years establishing a reputation, building a brand so that you are able to charge a premium price for your product. Now suppose that for some reason (harvest too bountiful or perhaps an unexpected recession that leaves demand unexpectedly small) you find yourself with an unsold inventory. What should you do?[4]

Why not just try to sell more of your own wine at a lower price? Wineries spend a lot of money and time building brands, and they find it isn't easy to raise a price back up once it has gone down. Some wineries that cut their prices during the Great Recession found it hard to raise them again later, thus they have been forced to adopt a different strategy. They've created new offerings that are positioned at a higher price. The idea is that if wine drinkers hesitate to pay more for the *same* wine, perhaps they will be willing to pay more for a *different* wine. The simplest approach, of course, is offer an "upgraded" version—a Reserve Chardonnay that is priced a bit above the regular Chardonnay. This doesn't always work, however, and some European friends of mine complain that Americans have overused the "Reserve" gimmick to the point where a winery might have two bottlings—the entry-level Reserve Merlot and the upscale Reserve Reserve Merlot. Ha!

So some wineries have come out with new wine brands to fill that niche a bit higher on the wine wall, but establishing a new upscale brand isn't easy, however. What's another option?

BACK TO THE DUMP BUCKET

This is where "dumping" comes in. Dumping is the act of selling a product for two different prices—one much lower than the other—in two different markets. Keep the price of your fine wine high in the home market instead of discounting, then off-load the excess in a market you do not normally contest. This works, and can even be quite profitable, so long as customers in your home market don't discover that they are paying more than others, and especially so long as you can prevent the cheaper product from being imported back home in a "gray market" transaction, undercutting your domestic price strategy.[5]

Chances are that you've tasted many "dumped" international wines without knowing it because international price comparisons are often difficult and, for minor purchases, also practically irrelevant. In my 2013 book, *Extreme Wine*, for example, I reported that the lowest price that one study found for the popular French wine Mouton Cadet was not to be had in France, where the logic of low transportation costs would direct you, but in the United States. Was it dumped here? Yes, in the sense that it was sold at a lower price that reflected the lower brand-name recognition in the United States. And in another part of the book, I reported on an Australian nightmare where the wines that they were selling abroad at lower prices that reflected local market conditions were being reexported back into the country by ingenious retailers, undermining domestic sales prices. Great for Aussie consumers, but a nightmare for the producers, who found themselves the unintentional victims of their own dumping, essentially subsidizing the stores that were undercutting the normal price structure.[6]

FRED AND HIS FRIENDS

They say that charity begins at home, and I think that's true of dumping, too. You are most likely to find dumped wines right in your own backyard. The trick is to learn to recognize a bargain when you see one and to jump on it. I remember my first real encounter with a dumped wine. It was from California—a domestic wine for me—but there was an international connection, too.

Domaine Chandon was the first French-owned sparkling wine producer in California, and the occasion of its fortieth anniversary prompted my wife, Sue, and me to pay a visit. I've long enjoyed the sparkling wines and now also the still wines that are produced at the big facility in Yountville, California. One of my favorite memories of Domaine Chandon involves a mystery that I uncovered back in the 1980s. I was rummaging through the wine bins at our local Safeway and came across a colorfully decorated bottle of a still wine— Rosé of Pinot Noir—by a producer identified as Fred's Friends.

I was a bit suspicious because the price was so low ($1.99), but I bought a bottle and took it home, only to discover that it was delicious, both as an aperitif and paired with salmon. Yum. We shared our discovery with friends, and together, I think, we bought every bottle that the local Safeway stores had in stock. It was our perfect summer wine. We were happy to enjoy the wine, but who was Fred and were we his designated friends (and why was he dumping this nice wine under a made-up label at a bargain price)?

I guessed the wine's real maker because the fictional winery's location was Yountville. Who in Yountville would have enough Pinot Noir around to make a pink wine like this and then be able to sell it for such a bargain-basement price? Only one possible answer: Domaine Chandon. Sure enough, I was right.

Doing some research for a *Wine Economist* column about Domaine Chandon's fortieth anniversary, I discovered a crude black-and-white image of the original label on a trademark registration website, and I uncovered more details about the origin of the still wine in oral history archives at Berkeley.[7] Here's part of the transcript:

> Our first couple of years when we started, we were making wine at Trefethen. Our deuxieme taille, the last cut on our press, we'd never use for sparkling wine. Yet when you get to that last cut, as a still wine you have the appearance in the mouth of a little bit more body because there's more tannin in the wine, and the acids are a little less so it's a bit softer.
>
> We thought, "Gee, this is really pretty nice wine just to drink as it is." I forget now why, but we decided we wouldn't just put it on the bulk market, which is what we do today. I think it was partly because we were making sparkling wine, but it was going to take three years or so before it was ready to drink, so we thought, "Let's have a wine that we could enjoy ourselves." So we bottled some of that—a thousand cases or so.

So that explains how and why the wine was made. But how did it get its name—and who is this mysterious Fred? The oral history continues:

> Came time to sell it and we were just going to sell it to friends of the company and employees. Michaela Rodeno, who was then our v.p. of marketing and communications, came up with the idea of Fred's Friends. I guess it was shortly after Fred Chandon had been here on a visit. He's a very charming person. He took us all out to lunch, the whole group; we had about twenty people working then. As I recall at that time, he had promised which he later delivered on—

that after we had sold a million bottles, everybody would get a trip to France. Everybody was quite intrigued with that; I'm talking mostly about people on the bottling lines, et cetera. So Michaela just came up with the idea of calling it Fred's Friends.

It's a great little story and it was a great little wine. The best part is that I was lucky enough to overcome the hardwired prejudice against inexpensive wines and enjoy Fred's Friends while it was there. But is this just history, as the oral history suggests? Would the same wine today just disappear into the bulk market and reappear who knows where with who knows what label, perhaps blended with other wines? Perhaps the most common strategy in the wine trade is to go into the bulk market and sell off your excess to another winery that will either bottle it under its own label or perhaps blend it with other bulk wines to make a wine for a client, such as a supermarket chain. This goes on all the time—you would be surprised how much wine is not originally made by the winery on the label—but it happens under the consumer radar, for the most part. Nothing wrong with this—lots of products, such as coffee and chocolate, are blends of one sort another—it's just not how we are used to thinking of wine. The bulk market represents a great way to off-load excess wine without undermining your signature brand (or to acquire extra wine if your usual vineyard sources come up short). Bulk wine is a big business, and I will have more to say about it in a later chapter. But it's definitely not the only game in town, because many wineries want to get more for their surplus wine than dumping on the bulk market may pay.

SEARCHING FOR THE WINE DUMPING GROUNDS

If there are dumped wine bargains today (and there are), where can they be found? The key concept in framing a search is to remember that you don't want your high-price-paying customers to know that the same (or quite similar) wine is available for a much lower price. Once the cat is out of the bag, you will never be able to sell that wine at that price to those buyers again. Never!

One strategy, therefore, is to disguise the wine so that no one knows where it comes from. This means, of course, that you have to disguise it better than the makers of Fred's Friends did back in the day—the fact that it was Pinot Noir (a main component of sparkling wines) and came from Yountville,

California (where Domaine Chandon was the only sparkling wine producer), sort of gave the game away. In today's Internet-savvy era, you've got to be sneakier than that!

One approach is to call up Cameron Hughes, a California wine seller who operates on the négociant model. A négociant doesn't make wine, but buys it, ages or blends it if necessary, and bottles and markets it under its own label. Hughes has become famous for selling the surplus wines of possibly famous producers. I say "possibly famous," of course, because the true source of these wines is never revealed, even when some tantalizing (but ultimately inconclusive) clues to possible origins are provided.

Hughes built up a cult following and then a mass following during the Great Recession when there was a lot of excellent surplus wine for sale. The company continues to prosper today on the basis of continued high quality and a solid brand reputation.

Down in Australia, where wine surpluses continue, wine dumping also continues at the retail level but in a way very different from that of Hughes. Some surplus wine Down Under becomes what are called "clean skins." The labels on these bottles contain all of the necessary legal information, such as alcohol level, region of origin, and grape variety, but no indication at all of who made them. Plus, there is no Cameron Hughes-style négociant-curated brand. Its South Australian Shiraz 2012, for example, could be a great wine from a great producer who couldn't sell it all under its own label and didn't want to channel it into the bulk market. Or it could be insipid plonk. Pay your money. Take your chances.

I discovered another variation on this Aussie theme while walking through the big Queen Victoria public market in Melbourne. I couldn't believe my eyes when I saw the big stack of wine barrels at the ReWine market stall. The ReWine folks offer a carefully curated selection of wines that they have purchased in bulk from Australian producers. They sell them directly to consumers in the Queen Victoria and Preston markets—the bottles are filled from big oak barrels. You can't get more direct-to-consumer than that! Bring your bottle back to be refilled (like the beer "growlers" that are gaining popularity here in the United States, where local law permits them), and you get a discount.

The wines range from basic dry red and dry white wines sold at a low price to some very interesting products on up the line, including dry, sweet, and fortified wines. There was a nice Pinot Noir from the Adelaide Hills on offer when we stopped by. You get what you pay for in the basic range, we were told, as these wines are blends made for a particular price level like basic wines everywhere in the world, with more distinctive wines at the higher prices. Something for everyone, I think, especially for a wine economist like me!

THE OUTLET MALL STRATEGY

Another approach to the dumped wine search is to look in places where mainstream wine buyers might not go. It might be safe to sell off excess wine at a lower price if you've found a marketplace that is for one reason or another off the radar of the full-price buyers. This is, of course, the logic behind the original factory outlet stores that once were few and far between here in the United States but that now seem to pepper the landscape. The logic of the original outlet malls—full of factory stores selling surplus merchandise for a song—was that the person who might shop at, for example, a full-price Brooks Brothers or Ann Taylor store is unlikely to pull off the road in some isolated location to paw through piles of discounted clothes—they'd die before being caught like that! And so a safe dumping strategy emerged.

What is the wine equivalent of the designer outlet mall? How about Grocery Discount, a discount supermarket chain based in Berkeley, California, that started out selling scratch and dent and close to "best-by-date" products that other stores didn't want to handle. Now it has some of these products plus a fairly full range of standard grocery items—including wine—all at bargain prices. The target audience may be budget-stretched retirees and low-income families, but I have seen BMWs, too, in the parking lot of our nearest store. Some of the wine sold fits the classic closeout profile, but some of it is clearly dumped in the good sense of the term.

"Flash sale" websites (there are too many to list) are another dumped wine sales arena. These websites offer small amounts of often well-known wines at discount prices. But there's a trick. The wines are here today and gone tomorrow. Missed the sale? Too bad. The people who get the wines are the ones with the time or patience to check in every day and the credit card headroom to jump in when something good pops up. I know several winemakers who thanked their lucky stars for flash sales during the Great Recession. These days, however, I hear that the market has thinned out a bit. The problem was that the sales were so good that mainstream buyers entered the marketplace and, having become accustomed to the flash prices, balked at paying more at retail or from the winery. The flash sites that remain today must be well managed in order to make their sales without cutting the winery's throat in the process.

Outlet malls are instructive if you want to think about the problem of dumping wine. Fashion designers originally sold their surplus goods at the outlet stores, but when the stores began to be popular, I understand that some of them began to produce products specifically for these stores. They aren't expensive goods at a cut price. They are designed to be cheaper right from the start. Are they a worse deal than the original bargains? I'm not really sure. In some cases I suppose that they might actually be better values. But they are a different sort of deal. And this, of course, also happens with wine.

The generic name given is "second wine," and the optimistic bargain hunter's conventional wisdom holds that it is the same wine in a different bottle with a different label at a lower price. Or perhaps it is wine from barrels that just didn't quite make the cut when the first wine blend was made. Almost as good, but much, much cheaper. I have tasted many second wines over the years, and I can tell you that the quality varies. Some don't seem to be the same at all, but others are just great.

THE FRENCH CONNECTION

For example, the second wine of the Col Solare winery is a delicious value for about half the price of the first wine. It is called Shining Hill (an English translation of "col solare") and comes from the same vineyards. Col Solare is a partnership between the Italian Antinori family and Chateau Ste. Michelle of Washington State. Another second wine I admire, also from the Pacific Northwest region, is called Pétales d'Osoyoos, made by Osoyoos Larose, which began life as a partnership between wineries from Canada and Bordeaux but is now in the sole control of the Bordelaise side of the family. Pétales is perhaps more approachable in its youth but certainly delicious and a great surprise to anyone unfamiliar with the Okanogan wine region of British Columbia!

I chose these two particular second wines to stress a European connection, which is a bit unfair. A great many wineries release a second label. Some are well known. Stag's Leap Wine Cellars, maker of the red wine winner of the Judgment of Paris in 1976, the famous French versus California tasting, makes no secret of its second label, Hawk Crest. But others keep the second wine connection strictly under wraps. So why stress a European connection? Despite the fact that marketing strategies may seem more capitalistic America than artisanal Europe, there's a good chance that the French were the first to invent the second wine concept. And even if they didn't invent it, they seem to have perfected it.

Or at least that's the impression that I get from reading Benjamin Lewin's 2009 book, *What Price Bordeaux?*[8] Lewin reports that as early as the middle of the eighteenth century all four of the most prestigious Bordeaux producers of the time—Haut-Brion, Margaux, Latour, and Lafite—were releasing a second wine in addition to the *grand vin*, or first wine. The motivation then was to assure quality in the first wine and reputation for the château. In good years, it might not be necessary to make a second wine—all of the lots of wine made from grapes from different parts of the vineyard might be good enough to be included in the final blend. But in bad years? An all-in-one wine, if released, might have lower quality that would affect reputation and sales far into the future. So the solution was to "declassify" the weaker lots and blend them into the second wine while making a smaller quantity of higher-quality *grand vin*. Thus were created wines such as Les Forts de Latour (the second wine of Château Latour) and Pavillon Rouge de Château Margaux. Production of second wines was quite limited until the last part of the twentieth century, according to Lewin.

But then fashionable Bordeaux became even more fashionable, and the prices of the *grand vin* wines began to soar beyond the capacity of many to afford. What to do? The second wines (not to be confused with second growths, which are made by châteaux that rank just below the top on the complicated Bordeaux winery league table) were an obvious target. If you can get the style of the famous *grand vin* and almost the same quality at a much lower price, why not?! Especially if you despair that you will never taste the first wine at all. The market for second wines exploded, with some Bordeaux wineries seemingly putting the cart before the horse, using the reputation of the first wine to market the second and producing more of the lesser wine than the *grand vin*. Fascinating.

These days, Lewin says, second wines in Bordeaux span a spectrum from wines that reflect the original quality-centered "declassified" strategy of early days to others that seem more of an attempt to cash in on the first wine's reputation. Basically, these are wines made to be second wines the same way some clothing designers may make goods specifically to be stocked at their outlet stores. Thankfully, Lewin tells us, very few are strictly cynical marketing plays, but frustrated Bordeaux fanatics may be disappointed to learn that some of the second wines are what they think and hope they should be, but many of them are not!

BOTH SIDES NOW?

Money, taste, and wine are blended together in a complicated and maybe even unstable mix when it comes to dump bucket wine, and I can't really decide whether to rant or rave about the situation. Maybe they deserve a little of both. Dumped wine discoveries like Fred's Friends deserve three cheers— what a great pleasure when you stumble upon a wine like that! And I know that there are many of them out there today, not necessarily secret second runs released under cover of darkness by famous wineries, but more like carefully curated wines or wine blends crafted by négociants who have sourced good juice from overstocked wineries, either through personal connections or bulk wine brokers.

But once consumers know that some very good dumped wines are out there, we become easy targets for exploitation. Even if most of the Bordeaux second wines are very good—and I suspect they are—they aren't what most consumers imagine they must be. And few of us who buy the second wines are likely to ever learn our mistake because, of course, we are buying the seconds since we can't bear to pay the full cost of the *grands vins.*

Damn dump bucket wines. I love them and hate them at the same time!

Chapter 5

Treasure Island Wines

Desert Island Discs is one of the oldest and most consistently popular programs on BBC radio. The show's format is simple and direct. Each episode features a prominent figure who volunteers to be an imaginary "castaway" on a desert island. There is plenty to eat and drink on the BBC's fictional isle, but not much to do. The only entertainment will be whatever the castaway brings along, and not many choices are allowed.

On Thursday, January 29, 1942, the first castaway, comedian and actor Vic Oliver, was asked to choose eight recordings as his desert island playlist. Eight was about the right number to fill the available airtime but not many musical selections for a desert isle, so the point was that the music would need to stand the test of time and be entertaining or inspiring when listened to for the nth time.

For the record, Oliver's choices began with Frederic Chopin's Etude in C Minor, op. 10, no. 12, "The Revolutionary," and ended with Richard Wagner's "Ride of the Valkyries" from *Die Walküre*. The Chopin would prove to be a popular choice among future castaways, with 232 appearances so far at the time of this writing. The pianist Lang Lang; Deputy Prime Minister Nick Clegg; and writer, broadcaster, and nun Sister Wendy Becket are among the most recent castaways to choose this famous piece. "The Girl from Ipanema," performed by Stan Getz and Astrid Gilberto, is also among the all-time top castaway choices—very appropriate for beach walking. Beethoven's Ninth

Symphony is the all-time, number-one, individual musical selection, but Mozart is the most popular composer.

The program's format has changed only modestly over the years. Today's guests still choose eight recordings, but for many years now they have been able to add a book and a luxury item. Daniel Kahneman, a winner of the Nobel Prize in Economic Science, selected a thesaurus as his book and a reclining chair as his luxury item; good choices, I suppose, but not as interesting to me as the complete illustrated catalogue of the National Gallery of Art and telescope that were selected by Sir Mervyn King, governor of the Bank of England. *Top Gear* presenter Jeremy Clarkson picked a jet ski as his luxury. Vroooom!

Millions of listeners have tuned in over the years to hear actors, artists, musicians, celebrities, government officials, and, yes, even economists name and discuss their favorite tunes. I suppose that musical selections give us a tiny glimpse into a famous person's soul. It must be seriously intimidating to make up a playlist knowing that so many listeners will be judging you based on your eight—only eight—choices.

DESERT ISLAND WINES

Wine critics Oz Clarke and Jancis Robinson have both appeared on *Desert Island Discs*, so we know what tunes and trinkets they would choose. Bach, Elvis, and a cookbook of French provincial cuisine rated high on Clarke's list; Robinson favored "The Holly and the Ivy" and "Dancing in the Streets." Her very sensible luxury-good choice? A fully stocked wine cellar . . . and a corkscrew!

To the best of my knowledge, there has never been a television or radio show about "Desert Island Wines," which is a shame since the world is full of wonderful choices, and the problem of selecting just a few to live with for a year or more is just as difficult, even if, as the program's rules provide, money really is no object. A few articles have been written about possible desert island wines, and Jancis Robinson once volunteered that her choice would actually be a wine from a desert island—Madeira! But overall the desert island wine opportunity has not been seized. Wine has so much in common with music—it can be elegant or raw. It can be sophisticated or undisciplined. It can be elitist or just down-home folks. Music and wine actually stimulate some of the same areas of the brain, according to published research, so musical choices and wine choices could be related. Probably the reason for the lack of a desert island wine initiative is a simple matter of technology. It's easy to name a song and then share it over the radio, television, or the Web. Not so easy to give millions of people a taste of the wine that you are talking about. Perhaps Apple or some other tech firm will come up with an iWine-ish downloadable winecast. Can't wait for it!

TREASURE ISLAND WINES

If desert island wines are not a very hot commodity, Treasure Island wines absolutely are, but I need to explain what they are for you to understand. Treasure Island is the pirate lair that features prominently in the Robert Louis Stevenson novel of the same name. I don't remember any wine in the book— do pirates even drink wine? What would Long John Silver's desert island wine be? No, probably no wine on Treasure Island, but there must be pirate booty there somewhere, which means maps and searches and X marks the spot.

It's a treasure hunt, we call it, when you set off under uncertain circumstances to find something that might not be there or might not be what you think. A treasure hunt is more like fishing than shopping, it is about finding something, and the thrill that comes when you make a discovery is sometimes almost as great as the pleasure you get from the treasure itself.

Treasure Island wines are the wines you find when you are rummaging through a closeout bin or scouring the forgotten back pages of a restaurant wine list. Hundreds of eyes may have surveyed these same products, but suddenly you recognize the clue to the treasure and pounce. It's a great feeling— no wonder people go on treasure hunts. And no wonder retailers sometimes go out of their way to unlock the treasure-hunter instincts in us all. Significantly, some of the most important wine retailers in the United States are famous for their Treasure Island strategies and represent extreme examples of the money, taste, and wine world.

COSTCO AND THE TREASURE HUNT SYNDROME

People love to hunt for treasure, so you might think that a retailer who wanted to take advantage of human nature in this way would want to keep the strategy a secret, but you would be wrong when it comes to Costco, a

US-headquartered chain of more than 640 big-box, members-only ware-house stores.[1] Costco flies its pirate flag proudly, announcing at every opportunity that it offers a treasure hunt of values. I admit to a certain fascination with Costco, so please forgive me if I indulge in a bit of Costco data overload.

Costco is surprisingly big for a company that has fewer than five hundred stores in the United States and fewer than seven hundred globally. It is the fourth-largest retailer in the United States and, because of its operations in Great Britain, Canada, Taiwan, Korea, Japan, Australia, China (online sales only at this point via the Alibaba platform) and Mexico, also the fourth-largest retailer in the world. It employed more than 185,000 workers worldwide in 2013 to staff the stores and assist the nearly 40 million households and 75 million individuals who hold Costco memberships.

Businesses and households pay annual membership fees, starting at $55 per year, for access to Costco stores and services. Membership fees amounted to about 2.2 percent of total revenue in fiscal 2013, which was approximately the company's net income (a fact that lets you know what Costco is *really* selling, which is memberships!). In 2013 alone, members purchased 3.8 billion gallons of gasoline, 112 million hot dog and soda combos, and 69 million rotisserie chickens worth $368 million. They bought 4.2 million store-brand Kirkland Signature men's dress shirts and 114,000 carats of diamonds.

Oh, and they also bought $1.4 billion worth of wine in fiscal 2013, of which almost half was premium price "fine wine." Costco sells more wine to consumers than any other ompany in the United States, and it does it using the same treasure hunt strategy that is so successful in the rest of the store.

So how does the treasure hunt work? You can almost always find the quotidian products that Costco is known for, including bagels from the in-store bakery, frozen boneless skinless chicken breasts, coffee, walnuts, and almonds. But beyond these staples and others like them, shopping at Costco is a bit of a gamble. New products appear to entice and delight and then, *zoooom*, suddenly they are gone, maybe never to be seen again. You never quite know what you will find at Costco, and you can never be completely sure if you will find it the next time you visit. Unlike Stevenson's Treasure Island, there is no *X* on a map marking the location of pirate gold. You've got to search out the changing selection of goodies every time you visit.

Costco applies the treasure hunt principle to many of its product departments, but perhaps most successfully to wine. Costco's wine sales strategy is almost deceptively elegant. When you shop for wine at Costco, you normally encounter stacked cases of less-expensive wines ($10 or less as a general rule) arrayed in the same warehouse fashion as most other parts of the store. And there, nearby, in wooden bins or displays, are smaller quantities of the fine wines that cost as much as $100 and sometimes even more. During the Christmas shopping season, I have spied a third wine area with festive larger-format bottles at larger-format prices. All the wine is well priced, with a standard markup of 15 percent over cost for all but the house-brand Kirkland Signature bottlings, which are priced at 17 percent over cost. This is a much lower markup than regular retail sales channels, but, of course, most other stores don't charge a membership fee.

One secret of the Costco wine treasure hunt is that there are far fewer wines for sale here than at other retail outlets. An upscale supermarket can easily stock 800 to 2,000 different wine choices, but Costco seldom has more than 150 different wines. Why? Because sometimes less is more and a smaller range of choices can be appealing if they are well chosen and well priced. More to the point here, however, is that the strategy of running out of one wine and introducing another is not necessarily obvious if there are a thousand wines, but it is easier to detect if there are only a few dozens to choose from. And running out of particular wines and replacing them with something new is key to the treasure hunt since it trains wine enthusiasts to stock up if they see something they like and to come back again and again (and to renew that membership every year) just to see what new treasures they might find.

THE OPPOSITE SIDE OF A TREASURE HUNT

If Costco is the epitome of the wine treasure hunt, then what would be the opposite? It makes sense that that the flip side would be a completely reliable wine shop where you can always be sure to find the same products week after week and month after month. And, since this is wine we are talking about, the wines themselves would need to be extremely reliable, with the same taste year after year (without any apparent vintage variation, if you know what I mean). In other words, the opposite of Costco with its changing selection of often very-good-quality wines would be something more akin to the beer aisle in your supermarket, where Coors, Miller, and Bud are always the same (no vintage variation), and they are always just waiting for you to drop by to buy them. To contradict the Rolling Stones, if that's what you want, you *can* always get it.

There are, in fact, shops and supermarkets where buying wine is a bit like buying industrial production beer. Certainly, large-volume brands like Barefoot, Yellowtail, Woodbridge, and Franzia make a point to produce wine in a particular style year after year. And, of course, they are also very careful to be sure that their vast vats never run dry. The world might run out of oil some day, I suppose, but I doubt that it will ever run out of Gallo Hearty Burgundy, which has been in continuous production since 1964! An important segment of the market steers a steady course to this type of wine—Constellation Brands' "Project Genome" study (so named because it sought to sequence the wine drinker's DNA) estimated that about 8 percent of wine buyers fit this profile. They call them "Satisfied Sippers." Apart from this group, however, wine buyers seem to be drawn in one way or another into the treasure hunt, searching for unusual wines, high scores, bargain prices, or some combination of all three. Every wine retailer I know has a strategy of some kind to appeal to these treasure-seeking buyers.

So what *is* the opposite of the Costco treasure hunt? I suppose it would be a store that takes the treasure hunt to its logical extreme. That would be a place (a big place, I think) where you could choose from not 150 wines, as at Costco, or 800 to 2,000 wines, as at many upscale supermarkets, but you'd have your pick of maybe 5,000 or even 8,000 wines. Do such places exist? It is estimated that as many as 80,000 different wines are available for sale in the United States (80,000 SKUs, in industry talk), and I have visited many wine superstores that regularly stock a significant slice of that total. Two companies have embraced the über-treasure hunt model and are rolling it out across the land. Welcome to the world of Total Wine & More and BevMo!

BIG-BOX WINE

Total Wine & More was founded by brothers David and Robert Trone in 1991 when they opened two wine stores in Delaware. The company has grown dramatically and now operates more than a hundred superstores in fifteen states. "Super" is the right adjective to describe the stores, as they do indeed regularly carry in stock about 8,000 wines from all the world's leading regions, in addition to 2,500 microbrew beers and 3,000 different spirits. Stores feature temperature-controlled cellars, classrooms for various wine-tasting events, climate-controlled walk-in cigar humidors, and a walk-in beer keg room. The stores are spread in an arc down the East Coast from Delaware to Florida and then up from Texas to California to Washington State. There are gaps in the map because of differences in state alcohol retailing regulation, and the biggest gap of them all—the vast American heartland—will soon get its first store in Minnesota.[2]

Three years after Total Wine & More was founded on the Atlantic Coast, another superstore chain was born on the Pacific side. This was Beverages & More!, which now does business as BevMo! It opened its first store in January 1994 and had six stores in the San Francisco Bay area by the end of that year. The chain has grown to more than 150 stores in California, Arizona, and Washington State. The geographic reach is a bit tighter than Total Wine & More, but the range of selections is much the same, with eight thousand different wines on offer at each store.

BevMo! and Total Wine & More aim to fill the same market niche, but they are not carbon copies, by any means. Until 2014, BevMo! had its own independent, in-house wine critic—San Francisco-based Wilfred Wong—who rated more than three thousand of the wines, giving customers confidence in making their purchases. The customers also rate the wines Amazon.com-style on the company website. BevMo! has an innovative Vineyard Partners program that lets them source about four hundred different wines directly from producers around the world, shortening the supply chain and providing unique wines, in many cases. Total Wine & More has its own WineryDirect program that allows it to offer about 2,500 different wines that are produced and packaged exclusively for sale at Total Wine & More stores.

The emergence of über-treasure-hunt, big-box wine stores like these raises a number of questions. Why did this trend begin in the early 1990s, for example? And what sort of choice do consumers really have when confronted by these massive selections? The first question is easier to address, so I'll start there.

The early 1990s was a critical time in the development of wine markets in the United States and around the world. It was probably difficult to find eight thousand different wines to put on a store shelf in the 1980s. Since then, however, the growth in wine, wine consumption, and wineries themselves has been explosive. Add to this the fact that retail alcohol sales laws have been liberalized in many areas, and you have all that you need for the growth of big-box wine.

There were a little more than one thousand bonded wineries in the United States in 1940. The number fell to about nine hundred by 1950 and just five hundred by 1960.[3] The number of wineries then fell again and did not return to five hundred (half the 1940 figure) until about 1975. I think you could have put a bottle of every single different wine produced in the United States in 1970 into a modern BevMo! store.[4]

The winery count recovered to about 1,000 by 1980–1981, and it finally grew to more than 1,600 by 1990. Then came the growth years (which were also the BevMo! and Total Wine & More years), with the number of wineries nearly doubling to three thousand by 2000–2001. That's fast growth, but the wine surge was really only beginning. The Wine Institute reports that between 2000 and 2005, more than two thousand new wineries were added to the US total, about eight hundred in California and the rest in other parts of the country. Wine in the United States really took off—and hasn't looked back yet.

Wine Business Monthly calculates that at the start of 2014, there were wineries in every one of the United States, adding up to 6,565 total American bonded wineries. Add to this the 1,197 "virtual" wineries that sell wine that others produce, and you have a grand total of 7,762 wineries—about one for every different bottle of wine on a BevMo!'s shelf.[5] Quite a change in a relatively short time.

But that's actually only part of the story, because these are only the domestic wine producers, and 30 to 40 percent of the wine on US store shelves comes from other countries. In retrospect, the same period that saw wine production in the United States begin to skyrocket also witnessed a surge in global interest. For different reasons, and at slightly different times, the New World wine industries in Australia, New Zealand, South Africa, Chile, and Argentina all caught fire and began to channel wine into US and world markets. By the early 2000s, the number of New World import labels was increasing rapidly (not to mention more imports from Old World producers).

Australia's surge was a calculated move to increase exports of high-production wine. Government programs, effective distribution, and a favorable exchange rate helped their wines gain traction in the United States, United Kingdom, and elsewhere. New Zealand benefited from international investments—French multinationals like Möet Hennessy Louis Vuitton, and Pernod Ricard directed Kiwi wine into their global sales channels. The end of apartheid allowed South African wine to reenter global market channels after years of isolation. Free-market reforms aided Chile, which makes a lot more wine than it drinks, and so needs to trade. And Argentina, facing declining consumption at home, also looked to foreign sales. The devastating peso crisis of the early 2000s allowed that country's wine industry to reset itself in a more favorable economic climate.

So, as you can see, the world of wine has exploded in the period since 1990, and big-box wine retailers like BevMo! and Total Wine & More are one result.

HOW MUCH CHOICE DO WINE DRINKERS HAVE?

The choice of wines on offer at BevMo!, Total Wine & More, and others like them is a bit overwhelming—can you imagine any other kind of category of store where eight thousand different products ranging in price from two or three bucks on up into the hundreds of dollars are available? I can think of only one example—a store near Olympia, Washington, called Shipwreck Beads that sells more than 48,000 different styles and colors of high-fashion beads from all around the world.[6]

But how much choice do wine buyers have and how does this affect the money, taste, and wine tango that we've been exploring in this book? As I explained in Chapter 3, having no choice at all is undesirable, but at some point too much choice is too much, and looking for the perfect treasure hunt wine (X marks the spot) is more like searching for Waldo. The Treasure Island choice begins to feel more like the desert island choice. Or at least this is what can happen if you find yourself overwhelmed by choice and so fall back into the rut of buying the same few "safety wines" again and again, just as the BBC's imaginary castaways endlessly play and replay those same few discs.

How much choice do US wine drinkers *really* have if we ignore the Paradox of Choice? The answer to this question, according to a study by a group of

Michigan State University scholars, is that it depends on how you look at the question and where you seek your answer. The study is called "Concentration in the U.S. Wine Industry" and it follows up on previous research on concentration in the US beer and soft drink industries.[7]

If you look at the question in terms of the number of different wine brands on the market and varieties within each brand, then the answer is clear. US consumers have a *galaxy* of choices when it comes to wine. But if you look closely at the thousands of stars in these wine constellations, I am sure that you won't be surprised to see that there are several huge business "solar systems" with dozens of brands each: Gallo, the Wine Group, and Constellation Brands among the US producers, for example, and Deutsch and Winebow among the importers of international wine portfolios.

The wine world has its share of mega and mini businesses, and some of the megas are very large indeed, but the degree of market concentration is much lower in wine than in beer or soft drinks. So if you look at wine compared to beer, for example (and I suspect that this would hold true for spirits, too), there is a very low level of concentration—lots of different choices, even taking the biggest firms into account. The top five firms account for more than half of US wine sales, which is a lot, even if it is less than the corresponding figure for beer or soft drinks. Although the study does not provide any international comparisons, I believe the US wine market is much more concentrated than France, Italy, or the United Kingdom, for example, but less so than Australia. (In the United Kingdom, the critical concentration factor is at the retailer rather than the producer level because the big retail chains are so influential there.) The degree of concentration also differs depending upon whether you look at all wine, as this study does, or segment the market according to price, which is the analysis I prefer. The market for wines selling for less than the equivalent of $5 per bottle is much more concentrated than the $20-plus segment, for example. Most consumers make most of their purchases within a relatively narrow price range, and it's the diversity in that segment that matters most to them.

The Michigan State team found that the nature of your choice also depends upon where you shop. Some of the supermarkets and wine shops that they surveyed in Michigan sourced their wine from dozens of different suppliers, providing the galaxy of choices that the vast potential selection promises. But other stores—national-chain convenience or drugstores, for example—can (and frequently do) quite easily fill a hundred-item wine wall with products from just two or maybe three suppliers. The megas can easily provide foreign and domestic selections of all the main varieties at every relevant price. So choice is both narrower and different. This has an impact on wines produced or imported by smaller firms, of course, and also (according to an interesting study by Rebecca Mino) on local wineries.[8] Mino found that Michigan wines were far more likely to be available at Michigan-owned retailers than at the Michigan affiliates of national retail chains.

These studies are very interesting and fun, too, but the main thing I appreciate about the research is the question that it raises: How should we think about choice when it comes to wine? Does the fact that some of the megas have dozens of different wines in their large portfolio of brands diminish choice? Certainly not, if the brands have considerable autonomy when it comes to winemaking (like the "string of pearls" model that Ste. Michelle Wine Estates follows). Sometimes the vast perceived choice is real.

But that doesn't mean that there aren't any effects of industrial concentration in wine, as the national-chain-store part of the study indicates. Some of the national retail chains treat wine as they do other products and attempt to minimize the number of suppliers while maintaining choice. Choice is diminished when the availability of "mini" wines and especially locally produced wines is taken into account, and this would be a problem if these stores are the only choice for wine (as they may be in some areas). Apparently, we need a mix of different retail suppliers to assure that the true diversity of wine is represented on the shelves.

And so the question of whether our wine world is ultimately more of a Treasure Island or a desert island depends upon your point of view! Not many choices on a desert island, but you are thankful for each one. The problem of choice is much different on a Treasure Island, depending upon whether it's a Costco-style treasure hunt or the serious sort of search undertaken in a big-box drinks shop like Total Wine & More. I guess there is no simple answer because people, like the wines they enjoy, come in so many varieties.

Perhaps the key to happiness in wine is to combine the two. Take inspiration from the desert island and find comfort and maybe even inspiration in the familiar. But don't be afraid to strike out into unknown Treasure Island regions, varieties, styles, and producers, guided only by your instincts—and maybe a tattered pirate map.

Chapter 6

Sometimes the Best Wine Is a Beer (or a Cider!)

There's no doubt about it—I am a lucky guy. As someone who speaks at wine industry conferences around the world, I get to taste some pretty good wines. When the meetings end and the reception begins, it is not unusual for the winemakers in attendance to uncork some of their very best products for us to sip, swirl, and (sometimes) even spit!

But I'm not always lucky in this way. Like you, I also attend a lot of non-wine business meetings and social gatherings, and I run into the wine reception dilemma. Cost is almost always a factor for the hosting organization, and when due economy is observed the wines aren't always the best or most famous. Sometimes they are generic no-name wines from unknown places produced especially for the hospitality industry. They exist for one purpose—to fill your glass and give you something to sip, swirl, and . . . *not spit*, darn it. While wine industry events usually provide at least a few spittoons for the professionals to use, social and charity receptions give you little choice but to swallow the stuff. Which is maybe why I really like outdoor receptions in the summer, where I can use the lawn as my vast personal dump bucket when I must dump or spit!

I don't mean to get all Grinchy here, but as much as I enjoy wine, it usually doesn't elevate my experience at these events. Thus, I was scowling a bit when I looked across the room and saw an old friend smiling away. Why was Allan so happy? Because, as I think you have already figured out from the title of this chapter, he had discovered that the best wine is sometimes really a beer!

My happy friend was holding a cold bottle of craft beer. I think it was a hopped-up India pale ale (IPA). No doubt about it—Allan's craft beer looked to be more interesting and refreshing than my glass of generic red blend wine. Why didn't I choose the beer instead? So I opened my mind up a bit and went back to the bar. There were the same uninspiring wine choices that I had struggled to navigate, plus an ice bucket filled with four or five different types of craft beer, ranging from lager and Hefeweizen to Allan's potent IPA, any of which looked like a better choice than what I held in my glass.

Why do wine lovers like me allow ourselves to be exploited like this? Maybe we are just narrow-minded creatures of habit or maybe we have grown accustomed to settling for lesser quality in situations like this. Or maybe, just maybe, it is because this isn't a problem that is unique to the cocktail reception circuit. Maybe there are better choices than wine everywhere—in restaurants, at supermarkets, on airplanes—and I am just a bit slow to realize it.

Take a trip to your local upscale supermarket and try to think outside the box (and I'm not just talking about box wine). Pick a middle-market price for wine and then compare what you find with the similar price (per six-pack or 650-ml bottle, as you wish) over there in the beer aisle. I think you will be surprised at what you find and at how diverse and appealing craft beer has become as an alternative to wine.

It wasn't always this way here in the United States. Once upon a time, beer in America was a mosaic of regional producers, many of whom made distinctive local brews. But then Prohibition came, and many of the smaller breweries never made it back. Consolidation within the industry left us with just a few huge national or international brewers, each focusing on a common-denominator, mass-market product. International travelers might seek out the unusual small-lot beers they sampled abroad, but most Americans accepted Bud World for what it was.

Then the pendulum started to swing back. Tom Acitelli plots the return of real beer in his book *The Audacity of Hops*, starting with appliance heir Fritz Maytag's purchase (and rescue) of the Anchor Steam Beer Company in San Francisco in 1965.[1] Others give President Jimmy Carter credit because he legalized home-brew beer in 1979, making the first experimental microbreweries possible.[2] Let a thousand little breweries bloom, Carter might have said (but probably didn't), and eventually they did. It didn't happen all at once, and certainly no one did it alone, but eventually the United States became a brewing hotbed, with craft breweries and brewpubs springing up nearly everywhere local regulations allowed.

The beer wall of your local upscale supermarket here in the United States is now likely to be almost as complicated as the wine wall, with its import and domestic products and many specialized and seasonal brews. You might think this would be bad news for the industrial brewing companies—and it is to a certain extent; however, many big brewers now make their own crafty products—but craft beer is also a challenge for wine because, as my experience with Allan has taught me, sometimes the best wine could be a beer!

WHY CAN'T A BEER BE MORE LIKE A WINE?

So, is craft beer the next big thing in wine? No—not if you're asking if wineries are going to start putting in tanks for IPA alongside their racks of expensive French oak barrels. But yes, maybe, if you are thinking about things in terms of market spaces. The wine-market space and the craft-beer space are increasingly overlapping as craft beers infringe on wine's turf and low-alcohol wines threaten to do the same for beer. And if the common battlefield isn't huge at this point, it is certainly growing and warrants attention.

A true craft-beer producer, according to CraftBeer.com, the Brewers Association website, has three essential qualities: it is *small*, with annual production of 6 million barrels of beer or fewer; it is *independent*, less than 25 percent of a craft brewery is owned or controlled by a larger non-craft-drinks company; and it is *traditional*, making beer with a strong emphasis on traditional malt, not other grains such as rice, which has long been an ingredient in American Budweiser, for example. "Microbrewery" is the name we used to give these sorts of businesses, but craft beer is the official term now as the focus has shifted from the size of their tanks to what's in them. Craft beer has gained many of the legitimizing features of wine, including authoritative periodicals and websites, academic programs and studies, and even its own encyclopedia in the form of the 920-page *Oxford Companion to Beer*.[3]

Although by definition craft-beer producers are relatively small, the market category has made a lot of news recently because of its rapid growth, in terms of number of retailers who carry craft beers, and total sales. In 2012,

Nielsen, the consumer-survey firm, reported that it added 1,400 new craft-beer products to its databases.[4]

Rapid growth from a small base—sound familiar? Remember the Moscato boom? Moscato (wines made from several variations of the Muscat grape variety) surged from a small market niche to become the next big thing and is, according to one report, now the third best-selling (by volume) white wine varietal in the United States, after Chardonnay and Pinot Grigio and ahead of Sauvignon Blanc. Is craft beer the next Moscato? I put the question this way because the particular beer that got me interested in the wine–beer nexus was actually made with Muscat grapes. It was a 12-ounce bottle of Midas Touch from Dogfish Head Brewery that I bought for $3.50 at the Metropolitan Market up the street.[5]

Although Midas Touch probably wasn't made with wine drinkers strictly in mind, it is certainly being marketed to the wine-consumer base, and I have to say that its complex aromas and flavors (plus a wine-like 9 percent alcohol by volume) make it a beer that can stand up to many wines in a sip-by-sip comparison. The brewery says that "this sweet yet dry beer is made with ingredients found in 2,700-year-old drinking vessels from the tomb of King Midas. Somewhere between wine and mead, Midas will please the chardonnay and beer drinker alike." I can't really disagree. I found it very pleasing (and not overwhelmed by the addition of saffron, as you might expect), but this is clearly a matter of taste. Sue was less impressed, saying that it didn't taste like beer and wouldn't be her choice over wine.

Midas Touch is not alone in this beer-wine category. Washington State's Long Shadows winery has experimented with three fusion products that can sometimes be found at their tasting room. There is a Belgian Abbey–style ale made with Syrah juice from their 2013 Sequel wine, a British-style made with Sangiovese juice from the 2013 Saggi bottling, and finally Sour Ale made with Riesling juice from the 2013 Poet's Leap. Here is a tasting note for the Sour Ale. What do you think?

> The lighter more refreshing brew of the three, it's made with Pilsner Malt from Canada and Hops from Yakima, while hinting at a Hefeweizen-like cloudy turbidity. The addition of Riesling juice—from the Longshadows 2013 Poets Leap—gives it classic characteristics of meyer lemon, mineral, and orange blossom, while its Sour Ale base which is fermented using a yeast called brett-

anomyces has a signature sour touch with notes of banana bread and hints of toasted grain. . . . In many ways, it reminds me of Champagne, or even well made Normandy Cider (French Apple Cider), and comes in at 5% alcohol by volume in a 22oz bottle. Great with oysters and soft aged cheeses.[6]

The Long Shadows Sour Ale and Midas Touch are not typical craft beers, but they demonstrate pretty well what craft beer is capable of doing in competition with wine. It is a complex and interesting beverage that pairs well with food, just like wine. It tells a story that draws in the consumer and deepens the attachment, just like wine. Interestingly, complexity comes at a lower relative price with craft beer than with wine, which is something to consider. The difference between the lowest- and highest-priced grocery-store wines is huge—sometimes a factor of 50 or more—with a $2–$3 per bottle equivalent for a 5-liter Franzia box at the low end and $100 or more at the top, not unusual at an upscale supermarket. You may get a lot more when you buy at the top of the line, but you pay a lot more, too.

By comparison, the exotic product premium for craft beers is relatively low—a high-to-low factor of 10 or less compared to 50 to 100. The Midas Touch was a bargain at $3 in the sense that it was not very much more expensive than basic beers and ales. And even the most exotic cult beers (like the locally fabled Pliny the Elder) can often be found for much less than $20 for a 650-ml bottle. So the Screaming Eagle of cult craft beer can be purchased for the price of a good but not spectacular or especially rare bottle of wine. You can see how that might attract the attention of some wine drinkers, especially young ones. And I guess it has.

Craft-beer drinkers often display the same sort of insane devotion and geeky attachment that we see in wine enthusiasts, and there are even interesting beer-tourist destinations like Bend, Oregon—an old mill town that is home to fourteen craft breweries within easy walking distance of each other along the Bend Ale Trail. No surprise that Bend attracts some of my university students (and their professors) as a Spring Break destination. It is a well-marketed example of a growing trend—beer tourism—that mirrors a well-established similar feature of wine world. Tours, tasting, food pairings, and beer-maker dinners—craft beer seems determined to have everything we do with wine and a lot more since beer makers are not limited to one vintage a year. Brewers can empty their tanks and try something new every couple of weeks. So craft beer has a lot in common with wine and maybe a couple of advantages. Compared to wine with its single annual harvest, beer is a Château Cash Flow business. Cash Flow Ale? Maybe that's how beer-drinking Midas got his golden touch!

With these products more widely available and a growing customer base that is ready and willing to experiment, I think it is plausible that wine and craft beer will increasingly share market space, and we must take that competition into account.

AND THEN THERE'S CIDER

Let's circle back to that reception for a moment, with me and my sad red wine blend wishing that I were Allan with his distinctive IPA. What do you suppose Allan was thinking as he saw me scowling at him? You probably imagine that he was feeling a little bit smug about avoiding the reception-wine trap and enjoying a tasty craft beer, but you would be wrong. Because while I was wishing I had a nice beer, Allan was dreaming of the cider that he'd rather be sipping on.

For as long as I have known Allan, he has been a fan of hard cider, the lively beverage made from apples and sometimes pears and other fruits, which is so popular in England and elsewhere around the world. Allan always thought that one day Americans would get wise to the delights of cider—but when? His ski trips to British Columbia often included cider tastings—the British influence there is still strong, and cider is a popular choice—but somehow those ciders never made it across the border in sufficient quantity to form a critical mass. Now we know that Allan was just ahead of his time, because ciders, both craft products and those made by large multinational companies, have become a hot beverage category. Like the craft beers that they compete with for shelf space, ciders are attracting wine drinkers like me who find the price–quality combination attractive, especially compared with wines of roughly similar cost.

I knew about the cider trend from my wine-market studies—statistics for cider (but not beer) are tracked along with wine by some sources—and I was vaguely aware of the rising number of ciders for sale at my local supermarket, but the connection with wine didn't really hit me until Sue and I, along with two research assistants, headed off on a fieldwork expedition to the Columbia

Gorge AVA. Rich Cushman is a veteran of the Oregon wine industry, and we were interested to learn about this region from him, so we visited the facility where he makes wines for his Viento label and for Mount Hood wines.

The setting was as much orchard as vineyard because the big climate-controlled warehouse provided perfect storage for both wine and tree fruit. After we had talked with Rich for a while and tasted many of his wines, he drew us over to a corner where he was making something else—cider! A lot of the winery equipment sits idle for most of the year, Rich explained, and the apples and pears maintained their quality for months with the right temperature and humidity. There was nothing stopping him from making cider (and generating some cash flow) throughout most of year. It was still a pretty small-scale operation when I visited. He "bottled" the cider in kegs—the same kind of kegs that he used to package some of his wines—and he sold them to the same Hood River restaurants and drinking establishments, who were happy to have a fresh and distinctive local product to serve their customers (in addition to craft beers on tap, of course).

Winemaker interest in cider is an international phenomenon. In South Africa, for example, Cluver & Jack cider has emerged on the scene, made through a partnership between the Paul Cluver winery in Elgin and the Jack family that grows cider apples on their Appelsdrift Farm in the Overberg Highlights district. They also grow grapes and make wine. Bruce Jack's great-grandfather was one of the first to plant cider apples in South Africa. The cider is made at the Paul Cluver winery using the Jack's traditional methods. Suddenly cider seems to be everywhere I look in the world of wine.

Cider and wine may compete for customer attention, but they also form a natural partnership because they are both fermented fruit-juice products, a fact that was reinforced in my mind when I met Ron Brown when I spoke to a meeting of Pacific Northwest agricultural executives in Coeur D'Alene, Idaho. Ron's family grows fruit near Milton-Freewater, Oregon, in an area that is part of the Walla Walla Valley viticulture area. His grapes, grown on a distinctive rocky terroir, were so good that he decided to try to make his own wine, which he does under the Windmill label. And then his thoughts turned to cider, using the shared-facility concept that I saw at Rich's winery. Ron's Blue Mountain Cider Company makes more than 120,000 cases of cider each year—much more volume than his winery ships—most of which is sold by other cider companies under their own labels.[7] What I especially like about the family's Blue Mountain brand ciders—apple, pear cranberry, raspberry, cherry, or peach depending on the season—is how much they seem influenced by wine. Some of the ciders are "estate" products—produced using fruit from the family farm—and there are also single-variety ciders, Estate Gravenstein and Winesap, which steal a page from the winemaker book.

I didn't know about Ron's winery and cidery when I gave my talk at that meeting, but I could see his eyes light up from across the room when I mentioned an article in that day's *Wall Street Journal* about a big apple shortage that was on the horizon.[8] Not Red Delicious or Granny Smith or Honeycrisp. These were apple varieties that you've never heard of and would spit out in a second. And the cause of the shortage was the rise of ciders like Ron's. Many ciders are made from familiar types of eating apples that happen to be blemished and unpopular in the fresh-fruit market, despite their good taste, and are sold off for use in juice, cider, and so on. But high-quality ciders, going for terroir and taste, look for hard, gnarly, bittersweet apple varieties that give the resulting cider extra depth and complexity. According to the *Wall Street Journal,* "A growing group of hard cider makers are pushing their drinks as a premium product with the complicated taste and terroir of high-end wines. But to add tannins to the fermented drink requires bitter apple varieties that haven't been grown in large numbers in the U.S. for almost a century." That's the business that Ron is in, and he told me afterwards that he was looking forward to planting more of those special apples just as much as he loved working with his rocky-rooted grape vines.

We were fortunate to be able to tour the orchards and vineyards, which are in the Oregon part of the Walla Walla wine AVA, guided by Ron's son Andrew, who makes both the wine for the Watermill winery and the cider. He showed us the original test orchard for the cider varieties and talked about how some types of apples did better than others on specific sites. Craft cider (as opposed to the industrial product) will become intensely local and terroir-driven just like fine wine, he predicted. Everyone will start out planting the same varieties, but specific site characteristics will determine which apple varieties yield the best quality in each case, so eventually each area will become known for its best cider, a particular type, style, or variety. Just like wine. We came home with several bottles of the Blue Mountain Estate Gravenstein, Estate Newton Pippin, and Cherry apple ciders.

The Browns' ciders made me realize that many of the distinctive qualities we associate with wine—sense of place, focus on different varieties, and so on—can also be found in other goods and beverages. Once I started thinking about it, I realized that terroir, which I think of as a unique feature of wine, has been appropriated by all sorts of products. Now there are single-estate coffees and chocolate bars, for example, and Absolut has released a single-estate vodka! Oysters are not just oysters but frequently identified by the bay, cove, or beach where they are harvested, with diners invited to sample and compare. Those things that make wine special are still there, don't get me wrong, it is just that others have teased out those same qualities in their own products, which makes them a bit more distinctive and, by comparison, wine a little less so, especially to younger or newer consumers who are coming to wine for the very first time.

I thought that Ron Brown's cider was about as close to wine as anything not wine could be, but then I learned that I was wrong. Allan was in town and brought two bottles of a new cider that had caught his eye. It was hand-crafted, 2012 vintage-dated, oak-barrel-fermented-and-aged, made with a blend of organic heritage apple varieties from an orchard in Sebastopol in Sonoma County. Dry and complex, it ticks all of a wine lover's boxes right on down the line. But it is unmistakably cider, not wine, and a good value.

Just as I was writing the draft of this chapter, I received an e-mail query about what you might call the "Midas Touch" of cider—innovative ciders that would not just appeal to wine drinkers but are actually blended with wine. Here's a snippet from the Craft Brothers' press release announcing their William Tell Pinot Grigio Hard Apple Cider that gives you an idea of the product pitch:

> William Tell and Pacific Coast [another of their products] are both true craft ciders, produced from a five-apple blend of fresh juice from Golden Russet, Gala, Fuji, Red Delicious and Granny Smith apples. The Cider Brothers do not use apple or pear concentrate, one of the traits that separate their ciders from the mass-market brands produced by the large brewers and cider companies.

Sounds a lot like wine so far, doesn't it, with focus on variety and authenticity? But wait, there's more!

Their Hard Apple/Pinot Grigio Cider is produced using 15% California Pinot Grigio with their freshly fermented apple cider, adding a unique dimension of flavor complexity, body and food compatibility.

How was it? Clear, light, and refreshing, with unexpected acidity and great for a hot summer day. But, Sue said, recalling her Midas Touch reaction, it's neither fish nor fowl. Not wine but not cider, either. Is there a market for hybrid products like this? Perhaps. Crossover craft beers and ciders—beverages that drink like wine and appeal to wine drinkers, whether they actually have wine or grapes in them—are a hot beverage category today, and I think they will only become more popular in the future.

MONEY, TASTE, AND . . . WINE BEER AND CIDER?

So wine has a lot of competition these days, and I am thinking that those undistinguished reception wines are living on borrowed time, or at least should feel a bit threatened. For consumers, this seems like the best possible news. Anyone with a serious interest in wine, and by that I mean an interest that goes beyond the alcoholic content, will find that there are many more interesting options available that at their best can provide the same sensory and intellectual stimulation, often at lower cost. Look around, my friends, and drink up! I think younger consumers have already made this discovery, and those of us from earlier vintages need to catch up with them.

For the wine industry, the news is cloudy, but perhaps there is a silver lining. As I travel the world, I find that wine producers see themselves mainly in competition with their neighbors in the next vineyard or winegrowing region, and I understand the logic. Winemakers compete with other winemakers for customers, distribution-channel bandwidth, and retail shelf space. It's like that old *Mad* magazine cartoon of Spy versus Spy—white hats against black hats. But in fact, as I hope I have shown here, the bigger war isn't among wine producers but between them and the real competition, such as the craft beers and ciders that I have discussed here and the craft whiskeys, flavored vodkas, and a sophisticated cocktail culture that is so complicated that I would need another chapter (or maybe a book) to even scratch the surface.

This real competition has appropriated some of wine's complexity and authenticity and used it to produce very interesting and appealing new products, partly because of the enormous range of traditional beer and cider styles that exist and partly because they are freer to experiment and innovate along the Midas Touch lines.

How should the wine industry react to these potent new foes? As I have suggested, some of them, like Ron Brown, Rich Cushman, and Paul Cluver, have embraced the challenge. Wine and cider work together from a business standpoint. Others have pushed the innovation button, sometimes a bit too hard. There is nothing wrong with the recent trend toward new sweeter wines, which might appeal to a cocktail drinker's palate, or flavored wines that seem like a reaction to flavored vodka. Some wine people fear that they will debase the whole wine category, but this seems unlikely. But they are defensive tactics, don't you think? What will it take to secure wine's fortress?

I think positive innovation should focus on wine's diversity. There really is an undiscovered world of wine out there waiting for its cork to be pulled in a more public way. Highlighting particular regional wine styles, indigenous grape varieties, and unique terroirs can be a way to bring aboard curious consumers without crossing the line from wine to . . . what? To flavored alcoholic drinks? Prosecco is a good example of this possibility. Prosecco was our go-to sparkling wine when we lived in Bologna, Italy, a few years ago. Light, refreshing, inexpensive, delicious—Prosecco was great but not easy to find back home at that time. Now, of course, it is everywhere, and it has brought new consumers into the sparkling wine category. Prosecco is a great success, but it is far from unique, even in its own category. There are lots of sparkling wine types and styles from dozens of countries that would appeal to consumers looking for something different—for innovation. I know my Australian friends are waiting for the world to discover their deep, dark sparkling Shiraz, but to be fair they drink up most of it themselves at the moment, so there is probably not much left over for the world to share. A sparkling *red* wine? You bet! And although some of the entry-level wines are appealing mainly for their novelty, the best of them, such as Ashton Hills, Rockford's Black Shiraz, or the Peter Lehmann Black Queen, are simply delicious.

A recent trip to Portugal revealed another possibility. Before I left, I knew Portugal for Port, naturally, and light white Vinho Verde and some of the red wines from the Douro. So I was very surprised to be served a chilled glass of an orangish wine, Moscatel de Setúbal.[9] It comes from the seaside area near Lisbon and is made from the local Muscat grape variety. But unlike simple supermarket Moscato, it is given serious treatment, aged in tanks for two years after vinification and then in oak casks for five years more. It was body, tannins, flavor, and a long finish. And I found it on a local store's shelves for about $10. Moscatel de Setúbal was new to me—an innovation!—but one that is very old in the Portuguese tradition.

The world of wine is filled with gems waiting to be discovered. Winemakers don't need to concoct something new, they can elevate what is already there, and in so doing they will both advance the diversity of wine and fight the good battle with craft beer, cider, and the other alcoholic invaders. Sometimes the best wine is a beer, but wine can rise to the challenge!

Chapter 7

Bulk Up

Big-Bag, Big-Box Wines

Charles Dickens used wine in *A Tale of Two Cities* to symbolize the intoxicating spirit of the French Revolution. Early on, cause and consequence of that intoxication are both displayed when a cask of wine falls to the ground outside Monsieur Defarge's shop and the crowd rushes in, scooping it up from the ground in their hands and sucking it down. Blood-red wine runs through the streets in the same way that real blood will run later in the novel. If the metaphor isn't obvious enough, Dickens has one of the characters spell out "B-L-O-O-D" in red-wine "ink" on the wall. Evil times are ahead when wine fills the streets.

Since life does at least sometimes imitate art, I had to wonder what evil was lurking when I came across a story about wine flooding the streets in Seaton, South Australia, in March 2014.[1] Was it an omen foretelling an Aussie revolt? Perhaps the mixture of money, taste, and wine had become dangerously unstable Down Under just as in the French Revolution, but the wine was white this time, not red as in the Dickens novel. Probably it was only what it appeared to be—the result of a traffic accident between a car and a lorry hauling a giant flexible bladder that contained more than 20,000 liters of wine valued at more than 500,000 Australian dollars.

I told several of my friends about the Australian accident, and none of them have reacted the way I expected. No Dickensian analysis and not much in the way of sympathy for the drivers or the winery. No, the most common reaction is this: "What? Do you mean to tell me that there are trucks driving around on city streets carrying giant bladders full of thousands of liters of wine?" I can just tell that they are never going to look at an unmarked truck the same way again. Big-bag, big-box wine fever has now taken hold. If they ever actually find one of these trucks, I expect they will try to drink it dry. And they'll probably scrawl "P-A-R-T-Y" on the liftgate!

Box wine has grown to new dimensions. Big 24,000-liter bags in big 20-foot shipping container-sized boxes. Ever tried it? Oh, yes, you have! They are a revolutionary force, perhaps just not in the way you think. Let me start small and work my way up in volume.[2]

CHÂTEAU CARDBOARD

You are probably familiar with box or bag-in-box wines. These are the nearly ubiquitous containers that are increasingly replacing glass bottles on store shelves and on counters and refrigerators of regular consumers of wine. The technology behind box wine is sixty years old—the American chemist William R. Scholle invented the first commercial application of bag-in-box technology in 1955. The bags were designed to transport and dispense battery acid. Safety, economy, and efficient shipping were clear advantages, and thus a packaging revolution was unleashed.[3] These days, thousands of different products leave the factory in airtight bags inside lightweight cardboard boxes. If you have ever pumped a serving of tomato ketchup at a fast-food restaurant or drawn a cold glass of milk from a cafeteria beverage dispenser, you can bet that there was a bag and a box involved behind the scenes.

The first bags were obviously very sturdy if they could hold battery acid. Today's bags are lightweight and very sophisticated, with layers of different plastics and metallic films carefully crafted for each particular use. Wine first went into a bag, as far as we know, ten years after Scholle's innovation was launched. Australian winemaker Thomas Angove released the first one-gallon bag-in-box wines in 1965, but it wasn't until 1967 that bag-in-box really began to gain traction in Oz. That's when Charles Malpas of Penfolds Wines figured out how to put the airtight spigot on Angove's neat bag. Bag-in-box took off in Australia and then around the world. People tell me that the boom in Australian table-wine sales (especially white wine) is due in part to this innovation, which reduces cost and increases convenience while keeping the opened container of wine fresh. Château Cardboard was born!

Bag-in-box wines are often used in casual-dining restaurants and similar establishments for wine-by-the-glass or carafe sales. The bags retain their integrity for much longer than it is likely to take for a busy bar or home drinker to empty the container—the airtight bag and spigot reduce spoilage. Bag-in-box wines are extravagantly popular in some countries—I have heard that they now account for more than half the wine sales in French supermarkets, for example—but they have always received a bad rap in the United States, where they are associated with bottom-shelf plonk. Box wines were a sign of low standards and bad taste—or maybe no taste at all. I once persuaded a friend to bring a box of a nice Côtes du Rhône red to a faculty party. The wine was good, and I am sure that it would have been greeted with great pleasure if the glass-bottled version went to the party instead, but my friend caught flack from his snobbish mates, who unfairly accused him of being cheap, tasteless, or even both.

It's time to reconsider box wine. Box wines first appeared in the US market in the 1970s and were filled with generic bulk wines. They were perceived to be one step down from the popular 1.5-liter "magnum" bottles of "Burgundy," "Chablis," and the notorious "Rhine" wine. Some of these box wines were cheap, nasty stuff that acquired a frequently deserved bad reputation. But times have changed, along with many of the wines inside the box. Screw caps had a bad reputation, too, and look how their image has been transformed. We once associated them with low-grade swill, but fine wines eventually appeared under screw cap because winemakers were disappointed by the performance of natural cork and synthetic alternative (the New Zealand producers were in the vanguard of this movement), and we began to appreciate that screw caps have many advantages. Now screw caps are actually associated with *quality* for some types of wine, especially youthful whites, and no one expects to pay less or get less because of the screw-top closure.

Box wine is clearly on the rise around the world (especially smaller 1.5-liter boxes) and here in the United States, where it is among the fastest-growing wine categories. Here's the story by the numbers.[4] The biggest sales increases are in "premium" 3-liter box wines (selling for $10 per container or more). This market grew by more than 15 percent in 2013, more than three times the growth rate of the overall market. That's huge! Total sales of box wines still trail standard 750-ml glass bottles (sales grew by 5.2 percent in 2013) and 1.5-liter "jug wine" containers (2 percent sales increase) by a large margin, but the gap is clearly closing.[5]

THE REALLY BIG BOX

Premium 3-liter and 1.5-liter boxes are a seriously important trend—part of the democratization of wine, since the sort of person who buys it is often interested in making wine an everyday beverage, not something just for holidays and celebrations. But it is not the reason why the streets of that Australian town ran with expensive white wine. To understand that we have to bulk up—to take the idea of box wine and amp it up big time. Big-bag wine is all about saving big—saving weight, saving money, and maybe saving the earth, too. Here are the facts.

Wine is mostly water, so it is by nature heavy and difficult to ship—from a transportation point of view, those coffee people have a real advantage. They only have to ship the beans, which can be thought of as concentrated coffee essence. The heaviest part—the water—is added by consumers in the final stage of the product chain. Unlucky wine producers have to lug the water part around right from the start!

Before the advent of the standard 750-ml glass wine bottle, wine was shipped in barrels and clay jars and amphorae—whatever was at hand. Bottles are elegant, but they make shipping complicated both because they are obviously breakable and because they take wine's weight problem—the fact that you are mostly shipping water—and compound it by adding heavy glass to the equation. The heaviest bottle I have found in my personal research weighed in at 1,084 grams, or more than 2.25 pounds—and that's its empty weight! It was shipped to the United States from Chile. And, of course, the glass bottle itself has to be made and shipped, so the carbon footprint of a case of wine can get pretty big when everything is taken into account. I know winemakers who source their bottles globally (from China for inexpensive wines, from France for some of the pricier ones) and then sell their wines globally, too. I don't think it is impossible for empty bottles to cross paths with full ones returning home on two ships that pass in the night.

The risk and expense of ocean shipping constrained the international wine trade for many years. Handling the wine case by case or by the pallet—it is called "break bulk" down on the docks—got the job done, but it was obviously an imperfect solution. The advent of the modern standardized 20-foot shipping container didn't change everything, but it changed a lot. Now you could fill a container with 10 pallets of wine, which is 800 cases or 9,600 bottles. Safe, secure, and climate-controlled (if you are smart, since heat spikes reduce wine quality)—this was a very good solution to the wine shipping problem, and it is no surprise that the box helped the wine trade expand around the world.

The shipping container helped grow the international wine trade, but it also changed it a bit because it shifted the scale of operations. It was still possible to ship small quantities of wine via break bulk, but who would want to do that given container shipping's advantages? So businesses that could fill containers tended to grow, and those that could not declined in importance. The big got bigger because they could take fuller advantage of transport technology, and the small?—they had to find a way to cope with the new realities. Some very small wineries that could not reliably send containers full of wine to individual market destinations found themselves out of the export business. In other cases, the focus shifted to middlemen, who would fill wine containers with purchases from many small and medium-size producers. Some of these importer-distributors became as famous as the wine producers themselves because their skill in assembling portfolios of excellent wines effectively turned them into wine brands. Terry Theise, a specialist in Rieslings and low-volume "Grower Champagnes," is one such figure, and I admit that I will readily purchase any wine that I find with his name on the back label, even if I have never heard of the actual producer. The 20-foot shipping container didn't create this phenomenon, but it probably accelerated it.

THE BIG GREEN BOX

And now the next logical step is here—a big, big 24,000-liter bag in that same standard shipping container. That moves the scale up from 9,600 bottles per box to the equivalent of 32,000 bottles! Wow, that's a big box of wine. I've known about big-box wine for a while, but I didn't realize how big the big-box wine trade had become until I received a Rabobank report titled "The Incredible Bulk: The Rise in Global Bulk Wine Trade."

Rabobank's report focuses on the New World wine trade since 2001, and the change in the composition of wine shipments (in terms of bottled versus bulk) is dramatic. Bulk wine (the big-box stuff) accounted for about 22 percent of New World wine exports in 2001 (the remaining 78 percent was shipped in bottle). By 2013, the bulk share increased to 50 percent, with the bottles filling in the rest. That's more than a doubling of the bulk-wine share of New World wine trade in a dozen years, an amazing shift that is all but invisible to consumers.

What drives the shift from bottle to bulk in New World wine trade? The short answer is Big Green, but green in two ways. Green, first, in the environmental sense. Bottled wine is both heavier and bulkier than bulk wine (glass accounts for more than 40 percent of a standard bottle's total filled weight). All else being equal (a big assumption in wine economics), shipping wine in bulk and bottling closer to the final consumer should lower the wine's carbon footprint. This is especially true when, as I suggested before, many of the components of the final product, such as bottles, labels, capsules, and corks, are also shipped from country to country as part of an unexpectedly complicated international product chain that then culminates in one final shipment from winery to export center to import center to distributor to retailers or restaurant to . . . you!

Lots of miles go into every bottle of wine, and bulk shipping can potentially shave some off the total, but this is not guaranteed, since even a local bottling facility must get all the bottles and other stuff from somewhere. And, of course, you the consumer can mess up even the best environmental plan if you drive 20 miles to a store in a poorly tuned, low-mpg SUV in order to buy a bottle of wine for dinner tonight. Your personal carbon footprint can stomp out many of the savings made elsewhere in the supply chain. Tesco, the British-based supermarket chain that is the world's largest wine retailer, is reported to be particularly aggressive on the environmental Big Green front, with bulk-wine imports bottled in the United Kingdom in screw-topped lightweight glass for its high-volume private-label brands.

Cost is another green (as in greenback) factor, and there are also savings here. Rabobank estimates that bulk shipping yields an average cost savings of $2.25 per standard 9-liter case (they estimate total annual savings of $142,300,000 in 2010 compared with the 2001 level of bulk shipments). This is a very substantial savings for commodity wines of the type that often appear in private-label brand portfolios.

The movement toward increased bulk-wine exports started in the Age of Abundance in the early years of the twenty-first century, when a structural surplus of wine flooded global markets and it was important to move it as cheaply and efficiently as possible. The global wine glut is over, but annual regional shortage and surplus are still very important factors that drive the bulk-wine trade. Because of efficient bulk-wine transport, poor harvests in one part of the wine world can be filled in quickly with wine from other areas. In 2013, for example, a terrible harvest in Europe coincided with a record grape crop in South Africa. Bulk exports surged, going from Cape Town to Europe to fill the gap there and also to Russia, to replace the bulk European wine that Russian importers had previously depended on. The harvest pattern is different each year—those unusually poor European harvests and the pattern of trade they caused are one reason bulk shipments peaked in 2013—so bulk-wine trade patterns are difficult to predict very far into the future. What we can predict is that the Age of Abundance, with its constantly falling wine prices, is unlikely to return soon. Those days are gone; rising costs and tight margins are likely to make that $2.25-per-case savings even more attractive to producers now, especially as they scour the world for supplies of wine to supplement scarce domestic juice.

For vertically integrated international wine producers, the decision to ship in bulk and bottle in the domestic market is mainly about these cost savings. They pay less to ship the wine and pay lower import excise, too, since the wine enters the country at the lower bulk value rather than a higher bottled value. But more is at stake, as the Rabobank report notes, for winemakers who sell to third-party importers. In this case, bulk shipping results in a new division of value added in the supply chain. Bulk-wine shipment subtracts some value added in the producing country (even though the lower overall cost encourages exports, which can offset the loss) and increases value added on the receiving end. I have spoken to winemakers who were also concerned about the loss of control when they export in bulk.[6] They are concerned that they may not be able to guarantee the quality of the final product, something that risks undermining their reputations. Others are concerned because the growth of bulk shipping has gone hand in hand with an increase in private-label wines, which are custom-bottled for large retail customers, and some smaller ones, too. The brand in this case belongs to the store, not the winery, which makes some brand-conscious wine business executives nervous.

The standard 20-foot shipping container revolutionized international trade when it became widely adopted. I don't think the rise of "uncorked" big-box bulk-wine shipments is going to change everything in the same way the ocean container did, but I do think the effects are significant. The big bag in the big box makes it cheap and convenient for large wineries to source wines of a standard type and quality from every corner of the wine world, with cost a key factor. Push this too far and the wine involved becomes just another beverage, just another global commodity.

Where will the big-bag, big-box trend end? How will it affect money, taste, and wine? Sometimes it is useful to think outside the box in order to gain a fresh perspective on wine by looking at another commodity or industry for insights. I think apples have a lot to teach us in this case. Apple globalization has been going on for a long time, and in some respects it is even more complete than wine. Humor me for a moment, and let's see what we can learn about the impact of big-box wine by looking at tiny boxes of apple juice.

THINKING OUTSIDE THE (JUICE) BOX

Consider the common juice box. If you have children or grandchildren or pack your own lunch, you probably have these things around you all the time. Who knew that they embody an extreme form of globalization? Take a look at the list of ingredients. Here's what I found on the back label of one of the leading apple juice brands: water, juice concentrate—no surprises there. But look where the apple juice concentrate comes from: the United States, of course, but also Argentina, Austria, Chile, China, Germany, and Turkey. The apple juice concentrate that supplies the juicy fruit taste could come from any of five countries on four continents. Wow! *That's* globalization for you.

When I first saw the list of possible countries of origin, I reacted in the way a wine guy would—must be a global *blend!* There's probably some master apple juice blender somewhere concocting the finished product. "Too much German," I can almost hear him say, "Add more Turkish apple juice to balance!" But, no, that's not what's going on, as you have probably already guessed. It's about cost, not distinctive national apple terroir. The juice concentrate is a completely generic product (simply apple—not some particular variety of apple) traded in highly competitive global bulk juice markets, where cost (for standardized quality) is king and minor changes in exchange rates, transport costs, and trade fees can have big effects.

THE RACE TO THE TOP

As we consider the major increase in bulk-wine shipments around the world, you can't help but wonder if juice box globalization may be on the horizon, with wine becoming as simple and plain as the juice in that box. It may be a profitable business and it may even be a pleasant drink, but it wouldn't be the same, would it? And I think that this is one way that the big-bag, big-box trend is moving the wine industry. A race to the bottom? Perhaps, at least in the sense that all the bulk producers are pitted again each other to drive cost down, down, down.

But that's not the only impact of bulk wine, if my apple analogy is valid. An unintended consequence of the box has been to intensify the search for higher margins in other segments of the market. This has produced two additional types of global wine and that best of all possible worlds scenario—a race to the top!

I'm old enough to remember when Granny Smith apples entered the US market in 1971 (from New Zealand, as I recall) as a premium product. The Granny Smith was developed nearly 150 years ago by a grandmotherly Australian woman named Smith who discovered the natural cross in her garden and propagated it. Initially, I think, the appeal of Granny Smith was that it was a premium Southern Hemisphere apple that filled a seasonal market niche in United States. Now, however, Granny Smiths are grown pretty much everywhere and have lost some of their premium appeal. Highly integrated international apple companies source them from everywhere and distribute them everywhere.

Granny Smith globalization is not nearly so extreme as juice box globalization, but it is still quite dramatic. It reminds me of some of the bulk-wine trade today, where certain "fighting varietal" wine brands are sourced from all over the world. Product differentiation is based upon brand rather than appellation or country of origin—which can change from California to Chile to Italy and beyond from year to year—just like the Granny Smiths. But quality is very important, even if brand trumps origin as a signifier. I think this is where the premium 3-liter wine box comes in and, as we have seen, it is a hot category in the US market.

The best margins in the apple business today are found in what I call the "Honeycrisp" market segment, where innovative superpremium products command high prices. The Honeycrisp apple was developed by the Agricultural Experiment Station at the University of Minnesota to be an eating apple with distinctive flavor and texture profiles that consumers seem to love. Patented and licensed, it has been a very profitable fruit. The plant patent on the Honeycrisp has apparently expired, so production is increasing, and prices have fallen a bit, but the idea behind it is still strong. Plant scientists in Europe have developed new specialized patent apples to take over where Honeycrisp left off. My wife, Sue, is especially fond of Kiku and Kanzi, which I think are variations on the Fuji variety from Japan that were developed in Northern Italy and the Netherlands, respectively, and are grown in limited quantities here in Washington State. Honeycrisp globalization is about product innovation and product differentiation. Follow the money: the fierce competition and tight margins created by juice box and Granny Smith globalization have nudged the Honeycrisp and other specialty products strategy into the spotlight.

I think the same thing is happening to wine. The markets for generic bulk wines and "fighting varietal" wines (the vinous versions of the juice box and Granny Smith phenomena) are fiercely competitive, with razor-slim margins for all but the most established brands. Result? A race to the top shelf of the wine wall, with all eyes on distinctive wines with real character (or with compelling stories behind them).

Is there anything to be learned about wine by thinking about apples and wine this way? Or is it an apples and oranges thing? Apples and wine are specialized industries, but they are both businesses, too, and both have been affected by bags and boxes—both the little ones and the big ones. I'll bet anything that large quantities of apple juice concentrate are shipped around the world in the same big bags and boxes as wine!

Big bags and big boxes haven't just served to fill the little ones more efficiently, they have also intensified the segmentation of the wine market into distinct categories, where money, taste, and wine are present in very different combinations. Ironically, therefore, wine has become both more democratic and more aristocratic at the same time, and bags and boxes are part of the story.

The quest for green gold at the bottom of the wine wall has pushed the focus of creative winemakers to the fine wines at the top. Does this mean that masses and elites both benefit from those great big bags? What a revolutionary thought!

Revolution? That's where this chapter began. But big-bag wine is a revolution of a different sort, and logically it needs a different sort of propaganda. So when the revolution comes, if it does, promise me that you will scrawl "W-I-N-E" not "B-L-O-O-D" on the wall!

Part III

A ROSÉ IS A ROSÉ? MONEY, TASTE, AND IDENTITY

Chapter 8

More Than Just a Label

Wine's Identity Crisis?

Readers of Master of Wine, Tim Atkin's eponymous website on May 30, 2014, were surprised to see a photo of two very cute kittens staring back from the screen. Internet viewers are known to be suckers for kittens and cats. Funny kitten photos. Cute kitty videos. Cat cartoons and jokes. Apparently, we just can't get enough cats. In fact, you might want to go online for a moment and search for "cute cat videos." My search turned up about 311 million possibilities, each adorable and collectively quite addictive.

Cats, it seems, are so irresistible that perhaps they should be regulated but, as the title of the article by wine writer Henry Jeffreys asked, should cats be used to sell wine (and should we buy a wine just because it features a cat on the label)?[1] Cats are already thus employed, of course. Herding Cats Pinotage from South Africa, Fat Cat wine from California, Red Cat cellars, Black Cat vineyards, and Moselland Black Cat Riesling, which comes in a bottle that is actually shaped like a tall, thin, black cat. Irresistible? You be the judge.

The problem, according to Jeffreys, is that wine (like the Internet) is so vast and complicated with so many options and choices that it is hard to grab attention, in the first place, and to stand out and be remembered. So cats and other cute (and not-so-cute) animals are used to market otherwise critter-free wines. Is this a good thing? Doesn't seem like it, does it? Seems like is it kind of undermining the true identity of wine. But, Jeffreys writes,

> We used to make fun of people who asked for "the wine with the pig on the label" (it sounds funnier with a broad Yorkshire accent), but I'm not actually so different. I'm terrible at talking with my fellow wine bores as I find it hard to remember the names of producers . . . The sheer complexity of wine makes it difficult to grasp and if I, as a drink writer, get confused then what sort of chance does that give your average customer?

I would join the chorus making fun of buyers who look for pigs and other animals on the label, except that I plan to open a bottle of Goats Do Roam Rosé from South Africa for dinner. The name is a playful take on Côtes du Rhône, appropriate given the Rhône grape varieties used in the refreshing wine, and the label features the image of a goat more or less like the ones we saw when we visited the Fairview Winery in South Africa, where this wine is made. Nice wine? Yes. Easy to remember? Very. But is this how we should think of wine—a goat joke? Back to Jeffreys' column:

> Ahhhh, I imagine you're saying, this is where properly-trained professionals come in, the wine "educators"—which to my mind sounds like somebody employed to deal with dissidents in Maoist China—or the merchants with their wine advisors. But most people don't want to be educated or advised—they just want something that tastes nice and that they can remember. . . . Yet it's striking how few wine producers make good use of images to sell their wines. So many bottles have abstract vaguely tribal logos, trees or faux Bordeaux labels with a picture of a château on. How are you supposed to remember them?

Although I might put it differently, I tend to agree with Jeffreys about wine, wine consumers, and the role of wine labels. As I wrote in my 2011 book, *Wine Wars*, globalization has brought a world of wine to our doorstep, providing us with a spectacular array of wines and wine styles. But sometimes the choice can overwhelm the average buyer, who lacks advanced training in wine language and global vineyard geography. This is where wine labels can be helpful because, when done well, they can communicate key qualities in a memorable way and so aid both buyer and seller. When done badly (don't get my wife, Sue, started about the unreadably tiny print on the back labels of certain Chilean wines!), they do little to tell the story of the wine or engage with the consumer. Wine labels have a job to do, but do they need to become the vinous equivalent of cute kitty videos to do it? And what does it mean for the future of wine if they do? These questions and others like them prompt this brief investigation of what the quest for money is doing to taste and wine as seen through the labels that guide our daily purchases.

WINE'S IDENTITY CRISIS

The earliest wine containers weren't bottles, and they probably had no labels. They were vessels of various sizes and shapes that were used to hold wine drawn directly from the keg or cask. The anonymous vessel said nothing about the wine, so obviously its identity had to come from another source—the maker if purchased directly from a winery, or the seller if sourced from a local shop or middleman négociant. A label gives wine a particular identity, and that's why it is so important. It is important to the winemaker, who should care about what that identity is and how it reflects on her, and it is important to the contemporary buyer, who needs a reason to choose any particular product in an increasingly complex and competitive market environment.

But the label also creates a potential identity crisis for the wine. What is a wine's identity exactly and how should it be defined? Wine is wine, of course, like a rose is a rose, and doesn't change with its label, but once we start to endow wine with a particular identity, we change it a bit, at least in terms of the way we perceive it. So while a rose is a rose and a rosé is a rosé, a wine's label sometimes matters a lot.

There are many ways to think about wine and identity, and for this chapter I take my inspiration from a recent book edited by Matt Harvey, Leanne White, and Warwick Frost titled *Wine and Identity: Branding, Heritage, Terroir.*[2] The premise of this interesting collection of academic papers is that identity has become an increasingly important factor in the way that wine is thought about, experienced, and, especially, how it is marketed. Harvey, White, and Frost, Australian professors of law, marketing, and tourism, respectively, analyze wine and identity in terms of heritage, branding, and terroir—three flexible but useful "created" concepts. You might think that heritage and terroir are historical and natural phenomena, whereas brands are manufactured by marketers, but heritage and terroir are subject to the same storytelling factors as commercial brands and are perhaps more powerful because, unlike a created brand, they bring with them a sense of authenticity.

Once I started to think about this trinity of created identities, I began to see them in many wine labels. Terroir is featured on the label of one of my favorite Rieslings, Pewsey Vale's single-vineyard "The Contours" from Eden Valley, Australia. The label shows an etching of the vineyard, which is notable for the way it is planted on curved contours to take full advantage of the site. The terroir message is obvious—this wine is a product of place—but there is also a strong nod to heritage because the wine is designated "Museum Reserve," which suggests correctly that it is part of a longer line of special wines, and the label goes on to tell something of the history of the vineyard (originally planted in 1847) and how its wines won early success in England.

I think you can argue that Château Latour's label also establishes a terroir identity, but in a different way. The label features a drawing of the small tower that is the distinctive feature of this famous Bordeaux producer's vineyard. The vineyards themselves are not shown, perhaps because they look pretty much like we expect vineyards to look these days, with neatly trimmed, arrow-straight rows of vines. But the small building is a landmark and establishes an identity of place that other wines, no matter how close they might be in quality, style, or geographical proximity, cannot claim.

If terroir can take several forms, heritage, it seems, is equally subject to interpretation. The Buena Vista winery in Sonoma, California, was that state's first premium winery, which gives it a legitimate claim on history. Founded in 1857 by Count Agoston Haraszthy, the original winery suffered the ups and downs of the US wine world and eventually fell into disrepair from earthquake damage. Jean-Charles Boisset of the Burgundy wine family purchased the winery a few years ago and restored it to its previous glory, both in terms of the physical plant and with respect to wine quality. The labels reflect the heritage in several ways, especially through the use of historical typefaces that give what I would call an "olde-time" look to the wines. The signature wine, "The Count," features an etching of Haraszthy to firmly make the link to

California wine history. Heritage is what this wine is about, and the label puts this right up front.

Heritage takes a different form at Château Mouton Rothschild, where each year's label features a different living artist's custom-created work. The roots of the label design go back to the 1924 vintage, which featured a painting by Jean Carlu. Looking for a way to distinguish the wine's identity in the postwar era, the owners began the practice of annual label art in 1945 with a design by Philipe Jullian. Notable names in the years since have included Jean Cocteau (1947), Salvador Dalí (1958), Joan Miró (1969), Marc Chagall (1970), Pablo Picasso (1973), Andy Warhol (1975), Francis Bacon (1990), Lucian Freud (2006), Jeff Koons (2010), and even Charles, the Prince of Wales (2004).

I'm fascinated by the Mouton Rothschild labels because of the way that they identify and develop an artistic heritage that is at once modern and classical and that is uniquely associated with this particular wine. The labels are statements that use wine to express taste, and, of course, they also generate demand for the wines as limited edition works of art that transcend the beverage category.

TAKE A FLYING (FROG) LEAP

Harvey, White, and Frost identify heritage, terroir, and brands as three ways to establish a wine identity and therefore three ways to think about a wine label. Heritage and terroir seem straightforward in theory, but, as we've just seen, they can be pretty flexible in practice. What should we think about brands?

When you mention brands to a terroirist, you will often get a lecture about the evils of mass-produced industrial wines sold by large multinational corporations using brands, slogans, and gimmicks meant to appeal to gullible buyers. But, as Henry Jeffreys told us at the start of this chapter, the audience that is influenced by clever, memorable brands is a pretty broad one, and one that does not necessarily exclude people who know wine quite well. So we need to take brands seriously. If we think about a brand as expressing a wine's identity, then it is or can be a very useful thing. What matters is what message the brand and its label convey, how well it is communicated, and whether it is authentic. If all three conditions hold, then the brand works. If any of them fail, then we might have an identity crisis.

A good example of an authentic brand, just to show that one is possible, is Frog's Leap Winery, which is now located in Rutherford, Napa Valley, California. The winery got its start in 1976 when John Williams and his friend Larry Turley made a little wine at an old shed in St. Helena that had been part of a frog farm years before. Williams was working at the time at a then little-known place called Stag's Leap Wine Cellars, where he helped blend the Cabernet that was top-rated in the famous Judgment of Paris tasting. He borrowed some grapes from Stag's Leap and, when the time came to put a name on the wine, they picked "Frog's Leap" as a sort of inside joke (frog farm + stag's leap), but one that might have resonated for a different reason with Californians familiar with Mark Twain's story of the celebrated jumping frog. [3]

Pretty soon Williams and Turley needed a label, they asked around, and a friend recommended a young artist named Chuck House, who was interested in trying to design wine labels. House, who was as unknown then as he is famous today, sketched out four possible designs and presented them to Turley, Williams, and their wives. A particularly elegant image of a slender frog flinging itself into the distance was picked by a vote of 3 to 1 (John Williams was the sole dissenter). The label, with the clever and elegant design, was instantly popular with wine drinkers and art lovers, too. A copy resides in the Smithsonian Institution collection. And House was launched like the frog he drew into a career that included hundreds of wine-label designs and many other projects. I suspect his fee today is higher than the "couple of hundred bucks" and a few cases of wine that he received for the Frog's Leap work.

You might disagree, but Frog's Leap and its label work for me as a brand, even though I know that very few buyers will be able to appreciate the back story that I've just told you and they'll simply respond to the "critter" image. Frog's Leap wines are as elegant as the frog image suggests. The winery has developed in harmony with the natural image of the frog, which has taken on additional meaning. Williams has become a leading advocate of organic and sustainable grape-farming practices, even dry farming the vines on the estate vineyard so the natural image of the frog is not out of place with the reality of the business. Some of the winery's early neighbors might have thought that Williams and company were taking a flying leap of their own with their commitment to environmental principles, but the brand and the label have all converged over the years. Wine-label identity crisis? Not here! And although you can argue that a frog isn't as cute as a kitten, it seems to work just as well.

ANOTHER FROG STORY

As good fortune would have it, I received an e-mail while I was writing this chapter that announced a new label and look for a brand of French wine from Domaines Paul Mas called Arrogant Frog (the frog coincidence is unbelievable but true). Arrogant Frog was launched in fifty countries around the world in 2005. The label featured a smart-looking toad clad in ascot, smoking jacket, and beret, sipping a glass of red wine (Ribet Red, believe it or not!). The suave frog was meant to represent winemaker Jean-Claude Mas, and I suspect the joke (because the identity is all about fun) is that he might be an arrogant "frog" because that's how some people think about the French, but he sure makes good wine.

Arrogant Frog has been incredibly successful in part because the wine delivers value and quality (*Wine Enthusiast* named Ribet Red a "Best Buy") and in part because the fun approach and simple label passed the cute cat test—people liked it, remembered it, and came back for more. Special labels celebrated the Tour de France (frog on bicycle á la *The Muppet Movie* scene), the World Cup (frog playing keepy-uppy with a soccer ball), and Valentine's Day (Lovely Red, with a romantic frog couple). The possibilities were seemingly endless, and it looked for a while like the fun could start to spiral out of control. Surely at some point the marketing department's search for clever new label ideas would overwhelm the winemaking side of the story, and Arrogant Frog would "jump the shark," like Fonzie (Shark Jump Red?) and cease to be wine and become only a brand. It never happened, but the skeptic in me wondered if it could, and not just for Arrogant Frog, but for dozens and dozens of other wines like it.

And so I was pleased to receive the e-mail announcing that Arrogant Frog would have a new label, but this one was no joke. According to the press release, changes to the Arrogant Frog brand package involved redesigning the label to include images of the winery and estate vineyards, shrinking the frog and placing it in the vineyards, and closing the red wines with traditional cork instead of screw cap. Jean-Claude Mas's signature now adorns each label

"A major goal of the Arrogant Frog re-launch is to show that this is wine made in a place with long history, by a winemaker with a deep connection to the *terroir* and the region," according to the winery's US brand manager. "Even with the success of this brand, Jean-Claude feels there is always room for improvement—and helping wine lovers better connect with the origin of the wine they are drinking is very important to him."

"We launched Arrogant Frog in 2005 believing that creativity, expertise and humor would propel the brand to success around the world," the e-mail continues. "And we were right—our stylish French frog became widely recognized and beloved, helping us launch the brand in more than 50 countries," says Mas. "But now that our out-of-the-box approach has attracted attention, we want the Arrogant Frog packaging to better express where the wine comes from, our winegrowing and winemaking values, and how our work to enhance vineyards throughout the Languedoc contributes to making a great future for this wine region."

If I read the message correctly, it suggests that cute cats are great but they have their limits. Clever labels and creative designs can get attention, and they can take a wine a long way (a very long way in some cases). But there is a point where cute cats run out of gas, and if you want to take the next step—perhaps to more sophisticated consumers, perhaps to higher prices—then the identity of the wine may have to change, and pure brand, if I can call it that, needs to align with something else, such as heritage or terroir or, as in the case of the rebranding of Arrogant Frog, a bit of both.

BARE FEET, BARE BOTTOMS

I admit that I breathed a sigh of relief when I read about the brand redesign, but maybe I'm showing my age when I take comfort in the Arrogant Frog's embrace of French heritage and terroir. The conventional wisdom in the wine world, as reflected in a 2014 quarterly report from Rabobank, holds that younger wine buyers pay much less attention than previous generations to traditional markers of wine quality, heritage, and terroir, in particular.[4] What matters to millennials is how the wine's identity connects to *their* identities, to their friends, and with their lifestyle. Two wine brands are singled out in the report for their connection-making success: Barefoot from Gallo and Cycles Gladiator from Hahn Family Wines.

Barefoot is probably the most successful US wine brand of the last ten years, and it does it by breaking most of the rules. It is inexpensive but almost never the cheapest wine on the shelf. Although most Barefoot wines come from California, that link isn't a defining characteristic—the wines are sourced from various regions based upon quality, availability, and, of course, cost. The wines are made in very large quantities and entered in various wine-judging competitions, doing well enough that most display a gold medal sticker from some event. The label, since that's where most wine identity is established, carries the basic legally required data and a drawing of a footprint such as you would make if you were walking barefoot in the sand.

Barefoot's identity connects with people who aren't worried about where a wine comes from or how many decades the winery has been in business. Barefoot consumers think of themselves as relaxed and unpretentious, and they want to enjoy a wine that fits their chilled-out, surfer-dude attitude. Barefoot sales surged during the Great Recession that began in 2008, and I argued then that the reason was that budget-conscious consumers didn't want to think of themselves as needing to "trade down" to lower-priced wines because they could no longer afford them, they'd rather think of themselves as "trading over" to a more relaxed idea of wine. And Barefoot really fit that self-image. I still think I was right about the trading-over effect, but Barefoot's continued surge surprised me, and I think I probably missed the importance of that new generation of wine drinkers and their attitude towards lifestyle, wine, and identity.

If Barefoot is about being relaxed, I think Cycles Gladiator is about having a certain style or self-image and buying a wine that reflects that, even if there isn't much obvious connection to heritage or terroir. The label for Cycles Gladiator is based on a French bicycle poster by Georges Massias from 1895. It advertises the Gladiator brand of bikes by showing a winged bike being guided through a night sky by a flying, naked, red-haired young woman. The image is colorful and revealing enough to get the wine banned from store shelves in Alabama, but it appears to have nothing much to do with wine or winemaking. But it obviously connects with consumers who find the art nouveau style and unexpected name distinctive, exotic, and memorable. The brand has expanded with bicycle-themed Cycles Clement Pinot Noir and

Cycles Falcon Zinfandel, each with its own distinctive fin de siècle French bike-poster label.

I've singled out Barefoot and Cycles Gladiator because of their great commercial success, but there are many other wines that have crafted brand identities specifically in order to connect with a target market demographic. There is a brand of wine called Relax, for example—can you get any more obvious than that? The label spells out R-E-L-A-X vertically up the side of the bottle. I'll bet Relax appeals to Barefoot's big audience. Anew Riesling is another interesting recent brand. Anew—like starting anew or trying something new—invites consumers to be different, don't you think? An especially good message for a Riesling, which is traditionally a poor seller in the US market but has grown in popularity in recent years. I suspect that the Anew brand is aimed at young women, because it presents itself to the world in an elegant bottle with a diagonal design feature that reminds me of a woman's off-the-shoulder gown. The label itself features a stylish flower design with Anew in light-blue print. It looks cool, a bit sophisticated and, with its screw-top closure, instantly accessible. And it is very good wine as it should be, coming from Ste. Michelle Wine Estates, one of America's premium Riesling makers.

Relax and Anew and other "lifestyle brands" are carefully crafted to align their identity with consumers' visions of themselves. This would seem to be fundamentally different from heritage and terroir messages, but I wonder if that's really true, or if wine has always been about lifestyle and identity, and it is only that the way we think about these things has changed with the generations, new forms of communication, and that wine has had to change to stay relevant.

PARSING THE WINE WALL: *99 BOTTLES*

David Schuemann makes his living crafting wine labels and developing wine brands for some of the most famous wine companies in the world. His firm, CF Napa Brand Design, has worked on hundreds of wine accounts, presumably earning more money in the process than Chuck House did with Frog's Leap. He is the author of an informative recent book, *99 Bottles of Wine: The Making of the Contemporary Wine Label*, which takes the reader through just shy of a hundred wine labels and explains the process that gave each of them their individual identities.[5]

Consumers generally drink with their eyes and taste with their imaginations before they ever experience a beverage in the physical sense, and you won't be surprised to learn that reactions are different with and without a branding message or with the same wine presented with alternative identities. No wonder the art and science of labels is a big business. Shuemann's rules for "articulating brand essence" call for clarity, simplicity, and authenticity, with the goal not just of establishing an identity but of also encouraging consumers to connect the wine with their own lifestyle narratives in an "emotional journey."

The emotional journey reference caught my attention because it reminded me of the insanely successful wine-identity program at O'Brien Estate winery in Napa Valley. Each of the wines in the O'Brien portfolio is named for a stage in a romantic relationship, from Fascination Sauvignon Blanc to Attraction Chardonnay on (I'm skipping a few steps here) to Flirtation, Seduction, Devotion, and, finally, Reflection, a sweet wine that is mean to evoke sweet memories when one of the partners has died. Some winery visitors tear up when they taste Reflection, a friend tells me, having been led through the emotional journey of a lifetime. No wonder a visit to O'Brien Estate is rated as one of the top Napa wine-tourist experiences. Not every wine brand can have such an extreme effect on their customers, but a high level of engagement must be a goal for many.

Shuemann's analysis of ninety-nine wines shows that there is no one-size-fits-all approach to establishing a wine identity and that various combinations of heritage, terroir, and brand can be effective. Each of the featured wines seems to tell a different story that was developed in close collaboration with the wine producer. Sometimes the story line is clear to even a casual observer, and sometimes, as with the famous Frog's Leap label, it is more of an inside story, but the impression given and reaction taken matter more than an exact retelling of the wine's history.

Interestingly, the Cycles Gladiator label is one of the Shuemann team's designs, and I was interested to learn the story behind it in his book.[6] Although the label and associated heritage-free and terroir-free identity works very well, both concepts, in fact, are part of the brand's backstory. The wines come from California's Central Coast, which is a great place to cultivate wine grapes but is also a place where artists, writers, and dreamers have often congregated and worked (think John Steinbeck, and you will know what I'm talking about). It seems that the winemaking Hahn family had an idea to try somehow to honor the spirit of the place—the heritage associated with the terroir, if you will allow me to use those concepts loosely. The Bohemian feel of those French bicycle posters somehow seemed right—"a beautiful and arresting image of personal and artistic freedom," according to Schuemann. The wine identity struck a chord with consumers, that's for sure. And the rest, as they say, is terroir-brand-heritage history!

At the start of this chapter, I was worried that cute cat wine was going to take over the world and that the need to grab consumer attention was bound to undermine ideas of wine as more than another branded alcoholic beverage. Now that we have reached the end, I am still a bit nervous about this, but I'm feeling less anxious. The need to grab consumer attention in a cluttered market is not going to go away, but it seems that authentic design has the power to drive out cheap thrills, at least to a certain extent. Does wine have an identity crisis? Yes, of course! Did you ever meet a successful person who wasn't at least a little neurotic? But I'm feeling good about wine's ability to find itself, after all, and to help us find ourselves, too.[7]

Chapter 9

Wine Snobs, Cheese Bores, and the Paradox of Globalization

Simon Kuper is a global citizen, and so like a fish in water, he sees globalization from an insider's perspective. Born in Uganda of South African parents and raised in the Netherlands, he lives in Paris and writes about global sport and global affairs for the British newspaper *Financial Times* (*FT*). His 2013 *FT* column "An Everyday Taste of Happiness" is on the surface an appreciation of good food.[1] Paris has great food, Kuper writes, and he wonders at one point whether he would live in Paris if its food was bad? No, he'd probably stay—he loves Paris—but he had to think about it. Eating isn't just taking on fuel, as it might have been back in the meat-and-potatoes days. It's now a source of nearly endless variety and pleasure.

And it's not just in Paris that these daily pleasures present themselves. You can find pretty good food just about everywhere these days—even in places like England, which was once famous for bad food—and globalization is partly responsible. "Globalization tends to improve cooking," according to Kuper, and I think he is right. Immigration, long-term movements of people, means global movement of their cuisines, enriching the host country's food scene. Global tourism means that millions are exposed to foreign foods and food ideas, and they bring their new tastes back home.

THE GLOBAL CHEESE BORE EPIDEMIC

How important is this cultural cuisine mix? Very important, at times. In 2013, for example, British prime minister David Cameron declared a national culinary crisis.[2] It seems that his government's immigration policies were found to be undermining Britain's national cuisine, which is "curry," or Indian food, not fish and chips or pints and pies, as you might otherwise assume. The *Economist* reported that the inability of skilled chefs to enter the country was stifling the industry.

"Chefs have become like gold dust," says Enam Ali, a restaurateur and founder of the British Curry Awards. The *Economist* reports that visa rules require chefs to speak English and earn at least £20,300 ($32,500) a year, far above the typical salary for a curry house cook. While in theory experienced chefs are given "occupational-shortage" immigration priority, in practice few of the cooks are able to qualify. Result? A shortage of labor—and of the skills, techniques, and authentic tastes these chefs bring to the British food scene.[3]

When the prime minister's favorite curry house was targeted by immigration officials looking for illegal workers, something had to give, and Cameron pledged his support for a key British industry and promised to help curry restaurants keep their competitive edge. "Like any industry this one faces its own specific challenges and I know that there have been questions on immigration and getting chefs with the necessary experience. So let me promise you this—we will work through this together. We'll continue to help you get the skilled Asian chefs you need," he said, according to press reports, while speaking at the annual British Curry Awards ceremony.[4]

People power—migrants and tourists—are not the only ways that globalization affects the food you eat. You won't be surprised to hear that the global media play a role in the spread of the world's cuisines, too. Julia Child and Graham Kerr (the "Galloping Gourmet") paved the way in the United States for what is now a global media foodie explosion. *Top Chef. MasterChef. Iron Chef.* Nigella, Jamie, Gordon, Anthony—like Brazilian soccer stars you can probably identify, these celebrity chefs known by a single name (but here are last names for those of you are media-challenged—Lawson, Oliver, Ramsey, and Bourdain). Good news, mainly, according to Kuper's theory. He even admits that as much as he may not appreciate the global brand Taco Bell with its television commercials featuring *Top Chef Masters* celebrity Lorena Garcia, it is probably better than the Wonder Bread cuisine of the 1950s that it has at least partly replaced.

But he doesn't forgive everything—"The 'food renaissance' is indeed linked to class and therefore encourages status displays: the fastest-growing demographic category from Britain to China today is 'cheese bores.'"

Could you take Kuper's essay and replace "food" with "wine?" Almost. The parts on immigration (expanded to include flying winemakers and multinational interns who circle the globe at harvest time) and tourism would hold true. Global media have not yet embraced wine to the same extent as food and fashion, however. But the positive general effects (and boorish negative side effects) that Kuper describes would still hold.

ASIMOV'S GLOBAL GLASS

If Kuper sees globalization as a glass half full, Eric Asimov seems to worry that it might be half empty in his *New York Times* column "Europeans Stray from the Vine."[5] He starts with the sad news that wine drinking is in decline in France. It is way down in terms of quantity, and he is concerned a bit about the quality. The French now drink more rosé than white wine, and box wines have risen from 5 percent of the market to 30 percent, despite being banned in some regions. *Sacré bleu!*

What are the French drinking instead of wine? Just about everything. Craft beer, cocktails, and spirits, pretty much everything. Even when they drink wine, the French don't limit themselves to the regional selections that might have been their only choice fifty years ago. Now they seek wines from across France and Europe and around the world. The French are becoming more like Americans! And Americans are becoming more like the French, enjoying not only their own wines but (with Asimov's enthusiastic encouragement) drinking wines from France and around the world. Asimov has written in the past what a joy it is to live in New York City these days with the world of choices (of wine but also food and other cultural produce) that are available there thanks to globalization.

Globalization has costs and benefits, he concludes: "The benefit is better wine and more pleasure for all who are interested. The costs? Homogenized cultures and hyper-competition for the historic benchmark wines that put them largely in the hands of the ultra-wealthy."

THE PARADOX OF GLOBALIZATION

It is worth reading the columns by Kuper and Asimov and looking at how they intersect, agree, and sometimes disagree. I'm struck by the fact that they both find class issues to be of concern when it comes to global food and wine, for example—the curse of rich wine snobs and cheese bores. I am also interested to note the way that they both end up commenting upon an idea that I first saw in a book by Tyler Cowen, *Creative Destruction*.[6] I call it the "Paradox of Globalization," and I have referred to it frequently in my nonwine writings on globalization.

Cowen's book deals with the costs and benefits of cultural globalization, and it is one of the best globalization books I know. Much of the book is a demonstration that the global cultural mix is so complicated that it makes identifying a truly pure indigenous culture very difficult. Whenever people mix, there are both import and export effects. Your culture (food, wine, art, music, fashion, and so on) imports some of the foreign influences, and their culture takes away some of yours. Both are enriched, at least potentially, so long as neither side of the exchange becomes dominant. Cowen's book is both celebration of the benefits of cultural exchange and concern that we might not know that we have lost something precious until it is too late.

That brings us to the Paradox of Globalization, which you will recognize in both Kuper's and Asimov's essays. Global influences enrich our lives here at home. More diverse food, wine, art, music, fashion—you name it. But there's a dark side, too. The problem is that this globalization isn't limited to your hometown. Everyone—in New York, Paris, London, Mumbai—everyone wants to enjoy these global experiences. And they get them, but maybe not all at once, and the rich have greater access than the poor. You get the picture.

Which creates the problem that when you travel, you find that the quaint little villages (and village wines) that you imagined would give you that authentic foreign experience have been replaced, at least in part, by the same global selection you have at home. In short, home gets better, but travel becomes something of a disappointment. That's the Paradox of Globalization. As everyone's hometown becomes globalized, enriching our everyday lives, the world seems to become less foreign, less authentically itself, and that seems like a big loss.

The globalization paradox is part and parcel of the world we live in today, and though it may disappoint us when we see the French losing hold of a certain idea of wine that we associate with them, I think we can also take pleasure that Americans (and the Chinese and many others) are embracing the culture of wine. We can hope that the younger generation in France will discover its own idea of wine.

A final point to consider is this: food is far ahead of wine in terms of its global diffusion and penetration, don't you think? The media's embrace of food might be responsible for this, but there are other factors—everyone eats but only some of us (the lucky ones) drink wine. But I think wine will catch up. Looking at the world of food today, I wonder what the world of wine will look like in fifty years?

THE GRAPE TRANSFORMATION

Wine illustrates quite well the costs and benefits of the global import-export mix. The early European colonists of the New World brought their wines and wine grapes with them and took the new grape varieties they found here back home. This backfired, unfortunately, because the New World grapes carried the phylloxera louse with them, which ultimately devastated both Old and New World vineyards. Ironically, phylloxera only became a problem when transport technology leaped forward. In the days of slow-sailing ships, the phylloxera-resistant New World vines dried out during the long voyage to Europe. Faster ships meant that the vines and the louse arrived in better shape and ready to do damage.[7]

The practical solution to the phylloxera epidemic was to graft Old World grapes onto New World rootstocks, and the vast majority of the world's commercial vineyards are thus planted with these "globalization" vines. You can still find "original" vines—European grapes grown on their own rootstocks—but ironically you are most likely to discover them in particular New World locations, such as Chile, eastern Washington State, and some parts of Australia, where the combination of very dry climate and sandy soil have thus far, at least, discouraged the very aggressive phylloxera bug.

Globalization in its pre-1900 forms thus spread wine around the world, nearly destroyed it, and then managed to save it again. Talk about a complicated relationship. Although the threat of phylloxera will never completely disappear (the louse seems able to evolve and adapt to maintain a constant threat), I think that concern about globalization has shifted to the rising influence of the so-called international varieties at the expense of indigenous grape types.

Let's see how much the international variety trend has influenced your experience of wine. How many different wine-grape varieties can you name? Seriously, take a moment and try to write down as many varieties as you can, starting with A (Aligoté? Alicante Bouschet? Aleatico?) all the way to Z (Zinfandel—that's easy). I wonder how many you can name. Some of the names come easily, but others are harder to tease out because they don't always show up on the wine label. Many Old World wines are identified by region rather than grape variety, but this is changing because, in part, of the international variety effect.

Did you manage to list a hundred different grape varieties? If so, and if you've actually tasted wines from all these vines, you are eligible to join a global band of 890 men and 488 women who were members of the Wine Century Club on the day I checked their website.[8]

A hundred grape varieties seems like a lot of diversity in the world of wine, and it is, but we are just scratching the surface. The 2012 book *Wine Grapes*, by Jancis Robinson, Julia Harding, and José Vouillamoz, lists a total of 1,368 different wine-grape varieties along with their history, genetic profile, and tasting notes. Incredibly, there are almost one hundred wine-grape varieties that begin with the letter *A*, starting with Abbuoto (an Italian blending grape from Lazio, near Rome) and ending with Azal (from Portugal). So getting that "A" grape list is more complicated than you might have thought. The "Z" end of the alphabet is harder, too, because the authors tell us that the Zinfandel that you thought was a safe bet is really a grape called Tribidrag that originated in Croatia. Stumped for a way to end your alphabetical list? You shouldn't be—there are twenty-two wine grapes that begin with the letter *Z*, starting with Serbia's Začinak and ending with Zweigelt, a red variety that is widely planted in Austria.

So there are plenty of grape varieties and corresponding wines in the world—globalization opens the door (in theory) to a cornucopia of vinous diversity. But what about diversity in practice? Ah, that's the problem. As contemporary globalization has progressed, certain money-driven international market norms have emerged. If you want to be able to sell your wine locally in, say, Serbia, then perhaps using Začinak grapes is no disadvantage. But if you aspire to taking on the world markets, then there is some pressure to pull up Začinak and plant something that is more widely understood and appreciated. Merlot, perhaps, or Chardonnay, or one of the grapes on the international varieties list that starts with Cabernet Sauvignon, Merlot, Syrah, Pinot Noir, Chardonnay, Sauvignon Blanc, and Riesling and moves on from there. Some people say that winemakers are pulled towards the international varieties by market forces. I have also heard it said that the market is just an excuse trotted out by mediocre winemakers. They blame the indigenous grapes (and not their own poor choices) when they make poor wines from them that don't find a ready market. Either way (or both ways) the result is the same—the diversity of choice seems to be diminished.

How strong is the trend away from indigenous grapes associated with a particular place towards international grape varieties that are grown almost everywhere and sold almost everywhere? A 2013 study by Kym Anderson and Nanda Aryal of the University of Adelaide's Wine Economics Research Center tells the story.[9] Approximately half of the world's vineyards were planted with about twenty-two different wine-grape varieties back in 2000, with the top five varieties accounting for 25 percent of total plantings. The other 1,300-plus grape varieties made up the rest of the world's vineyards.

Fast forward ten years—not a long time in vineyard terms—and the top five varieties' share of world vineyards has risen from 25 to about 30 percent. And just sixteen or seventeen grape varieties (not twenty-two as before) together occupy half the world's vineyards. The incredible diversity of the world of wine seems to be fading away!

What's coming and going? The University of Adelaide study finds that the biggest loser between 2000 and 2010 is Airén, a white grape variety used to make simple wines and as the base wine for brandy. Have you heard of it? Incredibly, Airén occupies the largest vineyard area of any wine grape in the world, with most of it planted in Spain. Other grape varieties that have suffered a decline include Mazuelo (a.k.a. Carignan), Graševina, Garnacha Tinta, Trebbiano Toscano, Bobal, Catarratto Bianco, Cayetana Blanca, Pamid, and Cinsault. The biggest winner of the shift to international varieties is Tempranillo (a quality Spanish variety), followed by Syrah, Cabernet Sauvignon, Merlot, Chardonnay, Sauvignon Blanc, Pinot Noir, and Pinot Gris. I'll bet that some of the "loser" grape varieties are unfamiliar to you, but all of the "winners" are wines that you would recognize. That's how the globalization effect works. Should we be upset?

QUANTITIES AND QUALITIES

Wine writer and former science editor Jamie Goode responded to the University of Adelaide study by wondering why we should be concerned about the internationalization of grape varieties.[10] Yes, grape variety matters a lot for basic wines, the ones that fill the lower shelves of the supermarkets. Global sourcing of bulk wines, shipped in ocean-going containers that contain huge 24,000-liter wine-filled bladders, is likely to require a high degree of standardization.

But what about fine wine, Goode asks? This is where matters become a bit more complicated. In the Old World style, Goode argues that terroir rather than variety is the defining characteristic. He cites Burgundy, where everything seems to be either Pinot Noir or Chardonnay, with few other options. A recipe for boring homogeneity from the point of view of grape variety. And yet the wines themselves are incredibly diverse and interesting and have inspired generations of wine lovers to study—almost to worship—the differences. What accounts for this paradox? The individual vineyard sites that are responsible for the wines.

Goode seems to believe that—for fine wine, at least—the importance of grape variety (and so the concern over globalization's effect) is overstated: "If you have great vineyard soil and a suitable climate, then you just need one or a few appropriate varieties to express this. Of course, we are talking about high-end wine here. The varietal story is the most important, I guess, for cheap wine." But, he continues,

> If you have boring soils or an unsuitable climate, you can plant the world's most exotic varieties, rescued from extinction, but it doesn't mean you'll have interesting wines. . . . So while there's a geeky part of me that delights in the thousands of grape varieties grown worldwide, as long as we have a few dozen of the best available, we shouldn't be in danger of running out of interesting wine any time soon, because it is the geography, not the grapes, that makes wine interesting.

THREE-SIDED VINEYARD

So does a problem really exist? Not if you take Jamie Goode's point of view that what matters are fine terroir wines. But while I respect his position, I can't bring myself to be as confident as he is about this. Part of this is quite simply that a lot of the wines I write about and drink myself are a good deal more pedestrian than top-tier Domaines Trop Cher Bourgogne. I'd be very unhappy if they lost some of the diversity, whatever its source.

Grapes varieties and terroir seem to be two sides of the vineyard coin that give us opposing advice regarding globalization's effects. What should we think? There's a third side to consider—the winemakers themselves and the techniques that they use. Does the lure of a global market cause winemakers to adopt a global style that may even overwhelm the diversifying effects of terroir?

Yes, I think so, but it's not necessarily a bad thing. Italy has an enormously complicated terroir, for example, and a long list of interesting and even popular indigenous grapes. But in recent years, whether in pursuit of global markets or just world-class quality, a number of important winemakers (Antinori and Gaja, for example) have radically changed the definition of their local wines through the addition of international grape varieties (Cabernet Sauvignon most of all, but also Merlot, Syrah, and others) and the previously uncommon use of new oak barrels. The wines aren't traditional by any means and often do not qualify for bottling under DOC (Denominazione di Origine Controllata). These wines, including the so-called Super Tuscans, bear the lesser, regional IGT (Indicazione Geografica Tipica) designation.

These wines can be very good. Indeed, some of them, such as Solaia and Ornellaia, are among the most sought-after and collectable wines in the world, selling for hundreds of dollars at international auctions. The Gaja wines, which come from Piedmont, not Tuscany, and so are not Super Tuscans but super in their own particular way, are in the same stratospheric realm. In a way (and this can be argued both ways, I think), they may have more in common with cult wines made in other parts of the world than with the traditional wines of their Italian regions.

THE PARADOX REVISITED

And so we come back to the Paradox of Globalization. We increasingly find the international grape varieties everywhere on the shelves where popularly priced wines are displayed. And we also find international-styled wines on the highest shelves, where cult or iconic wines hold forth. The differences among places in the wine world seem to be shrinking, even as the diversity of offerings within each region grows. Is this a net gain or a red-ink loss?

One of the readers of *The Wine Economist* (a blogger who writes as "Talkavino") provides an answer. Global food isn't headed in one direction, he says, but several. In particular, one movement is towards a sort of global fusion cuisine that draws influences from any, every, and all sources in the search for creative inspiration. This is Cowen's *Creative Destruction* taken to its logical culinary conclusion, where individual food traditions and techniques are broken down and reconstructed to create something vibrant and new.

But that's not all. At the same time, Talkavino tells me, global food is being taken back, back, back to its roots by locavore and farm-to-fork cooks, chefs, and eaters who seek freshness, locality, and authenticity above all else. A strong global organization—the Slow Food movement—exists to fortify local foods and purveyors against homogenizing market forces. Globalization isn't reducing the diversity of cuisines, it is simply changing the way that we think about and experience both the foods and their differences.

That makes perfect sense and reminds me one of Jon Fredrikson's sayings. There are no one-liners in wine, Jon frequently notes, it is never just one thing. Too complicated. Too interesting. And so it is with global wine, which seems to be moving in several ways at once with the international-variety bulk wines here, the locavore-terroirist Burgundy wines (and others like them) there, and the fusion-style Super Tuscans and their cousins somewhere else. What you see in global wine depends on where you look, how hard you stare. And what you want to see, of course.

Me? I want to see the diverse side of wine globalization, and I think it can withstand any challenges that the forces of commercial homogenization throw at it.

Now, if we can only do something about those damn cheese bores!

Chapter 10

Anything but Champagne

Ask a random sample of people what "ABC" means to them, and I think you will get a nonrandom response. The alphabet will surely be the most common answer—kids go to school to learn their ABCs. Music fans of a certain age might sing their answer—"ABC" is the title of a Jackson 5 song that hit number one on Billboard's list in 1970. Michael sang the lead.

If you ask a random sample of your wine-loving friends the same question, the answers you get might be a little different. ABC? A few will say "Alcoholic Beverage Commission," since that is a common name for the regulatory groups that set and enforce the rules of the game in many US state markets. A larger number will blurt out "Anything But Chardonnay," because that was a surprisingly strong trend in the wine world in the last decade. A certain rich, superripe, oak-driven style of Chardonnay that is closely associated with California and Australia became extraordinarily popular in the 1990s, and for a while seemed to drive more subtle Chardonnay styles out of the market. Perhaps inevitably the pendulum began to swing the other way, and some people announced that they had had as many glasses of sweet oak as they could stand. ABC—*Anything* But Chardonnay—was their motto then and for many still is, even though prevailing wine styles have changed a good deal.

But for a small minority there is one more definition: Anything But *Champagne.* As I hope to show in this chapter, ABC can have several different meanings when it comes to Champagne, which is an indication of just how prominent Champagne has become in the world of wine and in the world more generally.

WHAT THE FUSS IS ALL ABOUT

Champagne is arguably the most famous wine in the world. Certainly, many people who know nothing about wine—who couldn't name a wine grape or another wine type if their life depended upon it—can tell you a little something about Champagne, even if they have never tasted it themselves. It's that wine from France with the bubbles. Desirable. Luxurious. Expensive. And they are right. Champagne is unique in its fame and in the instant response it elicits. But what else is unique about Champagne? Let's break it down and see what we discover.

If you ask a novice what grapes go into Champagne they will often pause, take a breath, and offer a guess . . . *Champagne* grapes? In fact, I have seen some clusters of tiny grapes in the market from time to time labeled "champagne grapes," but they take their name from their resemblance to bubbles not their use as an ingredient in Champagne wine. Champagne is traditionally made from Pinot Noir, Chardonnay, and Pinot Meunier grapes used in various proportions: Blanc de Noir or Rosé Champagne blushes because of the red Pinots, for example, but Blanc de Blanc Champagne is *toute* Chardonnay. Mainstream Champagne is a blend of wines made from the three grape varieties taken from various parts of the Champagne appellation from several vintage years.

Although the grapes that make Champagne must come from the delimited region east and southeast of Paris, the grapes themselves are not unique to the wine. Indeed, Chardonnay is one of the most-planted grapes on the planet, and though Pinot Noir is much more temperamental and doesn't thrive in many regions, it is still found in various nooks and crannies on every continent, except Antarctica. I have tasted beautiful Pinot Noir from Burgundy, of course, but also from Italy, Germany, South Africa, Australia (both Tasmania and the "Big Island," as the Tazzies call it), Oregon, California, Chile, and Argentina. The basic ingredients are not unique to Champagne, but their specific soil type is not common—perhaps only sparkling wines from England share this specific terroir feature.

If grapes do not make Champagne special, then maybe it is the way it is made—*la méthode champenoise*, which involves a secondary fermentation of the bottled wine (responsible for the famous bubbles) and extended aging of the wine of the lees or dead yeast cells (responsible for some of the special aromas and mouth feel). This certainly is an unusual process and, along with riddling—the systematic rotation of inverted bottles meant to collect the lees in the bottle neck for eventual removal or disgorging—makes Champagne what it is.

In fact, however, the French do not have a monopoly on this process, but they do have a monopoly claim on the name of the resulting wine. Anyone can make a sparkling wine from the Champagne grape varieties using the *méthode champenoise*. Indeed, Möet Hennessy Louis Vuitton, the French luxury goods conglomerate, makes such sparkling wines in Champagne—and with local variation in California, Argentina, Australia, India, and China. The first sparkling wines in Champagne were probably made by accident—the secondary fermentation was unintended and resulted in exploding bottles until stronger glass, a British innovation, was introduced. (The British have a claim to the invention of Champagne, according to some accounts.) Early efforts in Champagne focused on eliminating bubbles, not creating them, until the glass bottle technological leap was made.

From a production standpoint, therefore, Champagne is not unique, it is simply a particular example of a type of wine made from widely planted grapes using industry-standard technology. And while the finest Champagnes offer a transcendent experience (as many of the world's best wines do), similar sparkling wines from elsewhere can be as good as or better than the ordinary product, generally at a lower price. Or at least that's what British wine critic Jancis Robinson once suggested.[1] So why does it get so much attention?

FOLLOW THE MONEY

It's the money, of course, which makes this a necessary stop on our money, taste, and wine tour. Although I won't deny the sensory and psychological thrills of Champagne, I'm also an economist and therefore trained to follow the money, as Deep Throat advised. Champagne gets our notice because many people have an economic interest in making that so. Benjamin Lewin broke down the situation in his book *Wine Myths and Realities*.[2]

What does it cost to make a bottle of Champagne? The grapes are expensive, but there is a circular logic here—the cost of the grapes is partly determined by the cost of the wine (which is partly determined by the cost of the grapes). Lewin estimates that the grapes that go into a bottle of typical Champagne cost about $10. The production process, with primary fermentation, secondary fermentation of the blended wines, riddling, aging, and so on, adds another $3 per bottle. Total production cost: $13.

But we are not through because there is one more item to add: marketing. Lewin estimates that promotional costs amount to an incredible $16 per bottle—more than all the direct production costs combined! Add to this estimated producer profits of about $5 per bottle and retail margins of $15 to $25 more, and you have a bottle of Champagne that sells for $50 or $60—a luxury product at a premium price. No wonder you know about Champagne. A lot of people—grape growers, wine producers, marketing agents, retailers, and distributors—have a strong interest in making sure you understand the magic of Champagne.

And so we come upon the first reason to choose anything but Champagne. Champagne drinkers pay a luxury tax that consumers of otherwise similar sparkling wines avoid (or maybe pay at a lower rate). Subjectively Champagne may be incomparable, but objectively it has many substitutes, some of which, at least, can be equally satisfying at a much lower price. And this does not even take into consideration other types of sparkling wines made with other grape varieties using the *méthode champenoise* (Spanish Cava, for example) or different grapes and different methods (the ever-popular Italian Prosecco). Taken together, the world is quite awash with sparkling wines, and some of them, such as Prosecco from the prime Cartizze zone, promise Champagne luxury at a more affordable price. Choosing anything but Champagne hardly restricts you at all.

ECONOMISTS ON CHAMPAGNE: A DIGRESSION

Champagne is special but hardly unique, and people, even economists (who are the topic of this brief digression), seem to have a love–hate relationship with it. They love the way it makes them feel. They hate the price they have to pay for that feeling. They love the tingle of the bubbles, but they don't always love the taste—when they bother to taste. I've led my university students in several tastings of sparkling wines, and I discovered that they were surprised at the taste of Champagne! I know they were not seasoned tasting veterans, but the fact is that they had previously just gulped it down—cheers!—and hadn't really given the taste any thought. When they did, they were stunned, especially when I asked them to spit the wine! Wow! The high acidity of the wine really caught them by surprise.

John Maynard Keynes loved Champagne. Keynes was possibly the most influential economist of the twentieth century—the man who decried the economic consequences of the Treaty of Versailles, diagnosed the causes of and prescribed the cure to the Great Depression, and drafted the outline of postwar international economic architecture at Bretton Woods. When asked if he had any regrets in life, he admitted to only one: not drinking more Champagne. Keynes even applied economic analysis to Champagne. Looking for ways to increase revenue from the bar at the Cambridge theatre where his ballerina wife, Lydia Lopokova, often danced (Keynes subsidized the theatre, so he had an interest in its "liquidity"), he studied the cross elasticity of demand between ordinary and premium Champagnes and proposed a novel plan to increase total expenditures by altering prices. Raising the relative price of the cheaper stuff would make the more expensive tipple seem a better deal, he said, and increase total revenues. I don't know if the author of *Essays in Persuasion* was able to persuade the bar manager to go along with the "up-selling" experiment.

There is no indication that the Father of Economics, Adam Smith, was fond of Champagne or even gave it much thought. Perhaps this was because of the difference in time and place relative to Keynes, but I think it might be because Smith was a *terroirist*. He believed in the idea of *terroir* and wrote in the *Wealth of Nations* that the wine grape was particularly sensitive to local growing conditions. He noted that certain famous Bordeaux wines earned a *terroir* premium in the marketplace.

If Smith was in fact a *terroirist*, he might have shied away from Champagne because most of the Champagne wines in the market place are relatively *terroir*-free. Yes, of course, they represent the *terroir* of the Champagne appellation. But the wines that come from the big houses are blends that come from hundreds of growers and several different vintages. The wines are made in the cellar and by the blending team at least as much as they are made in the vineyard. They can be excellent luxury products to be sure, but consistency is generally valued more than *terrorist* locale or vintage variation.

Grower Champagnes are different; both Smith and Keynes would love them. They combine all the luxury and sensuality that Keynes appreciated with Smith's intellectual focus on local conditions. Grower Champagnes are made in relatively tiny quantities by individual Champagne winegrowers from their estate fruit. They are cult wines, yet they are not always more expensive than the big house brands because promotion represents a smaller proportion of the total cost. So even the strongest Anything But Champagne advocate can make an exception for Grower Champagne, I think.

HOW CHAMPAGNE CREATED THE WORLD

Money, taste, and wine come together in an explosive combination when we consider Champagne. There are many reasons to love Champagne, and some to dislike it, and it is natural that different people will come down on different sides. But for me, the biggest factor is one that I haven't yet mentioned but that I can no longer avoid. How you feel about Champagne (and the Anything But Champagne pledge) may depend a bit about how you feel about the world—or at least the wine world. And this is the source of another Anything But Champagne experience.

Champagne has shaped the world of French wine, the world of wine, and . . . the world.[3] Champagne the region wasn't always the symbol of luxury that we know today. A crossroads of the north–south and east–west trade routes, it shipped its acidic pinkish Pinot Noir wines to Paris, the closest urban center. That market dried up when Fagon, King Louis XIV's physician, diagnosed that the regent's favorite wines from Champagne were the cause of his nervousness and gout. Fagon recommended he switch to the "pure" wines of Burgundy.[4] It took a while, but the eventual development of the sparkling wine industry in Champagne more than made up for the loss of royal court business.[5]

Wine became an industry in Champagne in the nineteenth century in part, I suppose, because the process is so very capital-intensive and in part because the wines were positioned as luxury goods, with the major houses vigorously promoting their private brands (Krug, Möet, and so on) and the collective brand of the region. High-fashion Paris and then fashionable consumers around the world became the target market driven by money, taste, and rising quality. Champagne reached its golden age in the mid-1900s. And then disaster struck—and struck again.

Phylloxera's long, slow, devastating, vine-destroying march reached Champagne in 1890, causing production of the prestigious wine to plummet. The solution to the vineyard plague was known by this time after much trial and error in other regions—replanting French grapes on resistant American rootstocks—but the destruction and associated cost was still crippling. Unscrupulous businesses found an easy way to refill the nearly empty pipeline—they purchased grapes, juice, or wine from the south of France and passed the resulting bubbly product off as real Champagne. Fraudsters benefited, but at a high cost to everyone else because quality was compromised and the collective brand—Champagne—was debased. When the French government sought to shut down the illicit trade, first in 1906 with a weak antifraud law and then in 1907 with stronger geographic designation rules, there were riots in the south because the small growers there saw important if now illegal market opportunities drying up.

Geographical restrictions—wine called "Champagne" could only be made from grapes grown in the designated Champagne region—addressed one problem (fraud, assuming strict enforcement) and opened up another—who would draw the lines and where would they be? A vineyard located inside the wine line would be worth much more because of the Champagne designation than one just 100 meters away but beyond the designated border. There were riots again, and violence too, this time among the Champagne growers and merchants, when in 1911 it appeared that the lines would be drawn to include a great deal of territory, simultaneously protecting and diluting the brand. When the final lines were drawn and a new postphylloxera golden age appeared on the horizon, other events conspired to bring the house crashing down. The fall of the Tsarist regime in Russia dried up the big Champagne market there, and World War I did just what you would expect by destroying consumer demand and grape supply at the same time as war raged on and the vineyards became battlefields. Fraud temporarily fell from the public enemy list, but not for long.

Hard economic times in the interwar years brought back the issue of collective reputation. Fraudsters could no longer easily pass off wines from the south as precious Champagne, but that didn't prevent the Champenois themselves from cutting their own throats by overcropping and otherwise undermining the quality of the wines they made at home. Each producer of substandard Champagne could gain a bit from higher quantity, but only at the expense of all of his or her neighbors, who found their reputation for quality correspondingly diluted. Left unchecked, the thinking went, quantity would certainly overtake quality in a rapid recession-fueled race to the bottom. Something had to be done to stop this and, because this is France, I suppose, the answer came in the form of public action.

Thus was formed in 1935 the INAO—the Institut National des Appellations d'Origine (now the Institut National de l'Origine et de la Qualité)—the government agency entrusted with setting and enforcing the rules of the game for Champagne, Bordeaux, and the rest of France's wine appellations, and also ultimately for many other products of origin, including certain special types of chickens, eggs, and cheeses, that eventually sought refuge under its broad protective umbrella. The INAO currently regulates 5,151 different products, according to the database on their website, including 4,441 individual wines and 58 cheeses.[6]

The appellation system was a defensive mechanism, meant to ward off foreign foes and domestic saboteurs, and it is perhaps not surprising how quickly the idea spread at a time when economic threats were seemingly numberless and promises of security particularly precious. And thus did the appellation system become the law of the land, first in France and then, eventually, everywhere. The INAO, with its definitions and rules became the model for policies of the EU that now protect the makers of Roquefort and feta chesses, for example, from unfair competition from makers of similar cheeses in other countries. And then, because that is how these things happen, the EU's products-of-origin system became part of the global trade regime of the World Trade Organization. The desperate defensive acts of rioting Champagne workers and merchants began a process that has led to regulations of global intellectual property rights. Nothing much stops people around the world from making wine that is like Champagne or cheese that is like Roquefort or ham that is like Prosciutto de Parma, for example. They just can't call them by those names. That's the law!

Perhaps because they were the first, the Champagne makers have been particularly diligent in enforcing their intellectual ownership of the name

Champagne. Or perhaps it is the influence of luxury-goods multinationals that own some of the big Champagne houses—they have considerable experience in fending off those who trespass on their trademark rights. In any case, no one seems to work as hard as Champagne to protect its identity, and I can't really fault them for this because it seems to pay off and because the idea that a local region can own both a product and its name is now firmly entrenched in both law and conventional wisdom. Even, as in a case brought against winemakers in the old town of Champagne, Switzerland, where the offending parties would seem to have a solid claim on their own patrimony. They may make sparking line in the Swiss Champagne, but Champagne it cannot be.[7]

More to the point is the problem of protected versus generic designations. In Italy, "parmesan" cheese has a specific meaning because Parmigiano-Reggiano is a protected product. In the United States, however, parmesan cheese by long use has a generic meaning, and I doubt that many people would mistake the inexpensive Kraft "spaghetti" cheese called parmesan for the complex luxury good from Emilia Romagna. But rules are rules, and the Europeans, having invented this system, seem determined to rub out all traces of trademark infringement, causing the *Economist* magazine to wonder where it all might end. What will the Europeans stake a claim to next? French Fries? Italian Dressing? Hamburgers? Is Champagne-inspired world dominance a "feta accompli?"[8] Ha!

I can understand the desire to protect a valuable brand, but I think that in the case of wine, perhaps excluding Champagne, the strategy may have backfired. Many New World wines once named themselves according to Old World regions, calling themselves Burgundy (for a lighter red), Chablis (for a drier white), or sweeter Rhine, for example, regardless of whether they contained any of the grapes associated with these regions and despite their lack of designated origin. This offended the Old World producers, but it didn't bother the local consumers, most of whom would never taste the imported real thing. But the Old Worlders pursued their rights vigorously under international law—so vigorously that the New World producers have little choice but to find other ways to designate their wines. So they built powerful private brands and labeled their wines according to grape variety rather than geographic region. The simple, new system found an appreciative audience among the new world of wine drinkers that globalization has helped create. The resulting New World *lingua franca* was so successful that the Old World has struggled to compete with it on international markets and now has begun to adopt the new naming protocols itself. Could Anything But Champagne have sparked a revolution with such unexpected results?

A CERTAIN IDEA OF FRANCE

I was first surprised and then delighted when Rebecca Gibb put me onto a book that revealed one final side of the Anything But Champagne story. I'm referring to *When Champagne Became French*, by Kolleen M. Guy.[9] Guy notes that the period of the Champagne's grab for special status corresponded with a time of intense nation-building within France. Although today we think of France as a unified state (or as unified as any democracy is these days), the people of France have long been separated by intense regional rivalries and cultural and linguistic differences—a fact made clear in Graham Robb's outstanding book *The Discovery of France*.[10] All manner of strategies were set in motion in days past to connect the many separate parts of the country and make them into a historical-linguistic-cultural-economic whole. Even the Tour de France bicycle race played a part in early twentieth century French nation-building by stressing the connections between and among the different regions.

In this context, Guy notes, the Champagne riots—first in the south when the illicit northern market was shut off and then, more violently, in the north when the appellation lines were being drawn—must have been seen as particularly threatening to national unity. Not just threatening to order, but a threat to the bigger project of creating a certain idea of France, to borrow a phrase from Charles de Gaulle. The INAO and its rules and regulations were obviously about division not unity, about how the benefits would be split or shared (or not). How was it possible to reconcile division and unity at a time of great tension?

The answer, Guy writes, was to create a special narrative about Champagne that only Champagne could sustain, to make Champagne not just a region within France, but France itself, sort of like Joan of Arc. Protecting Champagne (and all the others as the multiple divisions of the appellation system progressed) was necessary to protect the idea of France and was not, no matter how obvious it might seem, an act of pure economic self-interest. It was not an easy sell, as Guy explains, and I imagine that not a few people saw through the double-speak of "divided, we are unified," but the story held. It held well enough so that Champagne's particular place became part of the story of French unity. It held well enough for the division of the land and the establishment and protection of local product autonomy to became part of the process of the EU. And now it is global law, too, in a world where not too many laws span so many borders.

Could Anything But Champagne have accomplished all this? I think not! The money behind Champagne, its distinctive taste (and bubbly feel), and the way that these qualities were deployed to create a France that was united in its divisions—only Champagne could have defined the world this way!

Part IV

WHAT MONEY CAN (AND CAN'T) BUY

Chapter 11

Restaurant Wars

There are many tense moments on the television series *Top Chef*, a "reality" show where groups of talented culinary professionals compete in various elimination trials in order for one of them to emerge as the king of the kitchen hill. The hot-stove tension, exotic food, and outrageous personalities obviously hook television viewers. *Top Chef* was a hit right from its 2006 debut and, along with *Top Chef Masters*, *Top Chef Duels*, and other associated enterprises, has made celebrities out of the winners, some of the losers, and most of the judges.

Perhaps the most stressful *Top Chef* episode of each season is a team competition called "Restaurant Wars." Randomly chosen teams of the surviving chefs must work together to open a pop-up restaurant for one night. They have to choose the restaurant's name and menu, decorate it, purchase all of the glasses, dishes, and serving gear, train the waitstaff, and work the house. Oh, and they must purchase and prepare the food. The diners and judges compare the two teams' results and pick a winner. No one on the winning team can be eliminated, but someone on the losing team must go home, dreams in tatters.[1]

The trick to surviving the Restaurant Wars is not to be on the losing team, and that means working together with the very people who you fear are trying to throw you under the bus. Easier said than done, which is why this is the episode that viewers love and the would-be top chefs hate.

RESTAURANT WINE WARS

Love and hate. That's the way many wine enthusiasts feel about wine in restaurants. They love it, of course, because what could be better than to have a great wine with great food in a fine atmosphere, which might be a luxurious Michelin-starred, white-table-cloth establishment, or something much more casual. Food loves wine. Wine loves food. We love them both. What could be better?

But then there's the hate thing. There are so many things about wine in a restaurant that people seem to hate, starting with price and moving on to selection, service, and so forth, right on down to the temperature of the served wine (reds too warm, whites too cold) and even the type of glassware employed. Really, it is enough to make a serious wine drinker (or maybe a wine snob) stay home! And that's what many of them do, rather than endure the many perceived insults of restaurant wine.

"War is hell," we are told, and *Wall Street Journal* columnist Dan Ariely says that restaurant wine is hellish combat. "The first thing to realize when picking from a wine list is that you are in a battlefield. This is a battle for your wallet—a fight between the restaurant, whose interest is to get as much of your money as possible right now, and your savings account." And it's not an even playing field, either, Ariely says. "The restaurant's owners have much more data than you do about how people make their wine decisions, and they also get to set up the menu in a way that gives them the upper hand."[2]

Sometimes it does seem like restaurants are taking advantage of the complicated relationship among money, taste, and wine, using your love of wine to force you into a money or taste trap. If you want to satisfy your taste for fine wine with your meal, you will need to part with a lot of money. If you want to keep your money, be prepared to have your taste insulted. It would be easy to go into a rant about this situation—I can just hear it now, and it would include the line that the bottle of wine isn't the only thing that's getting corkscrewed at many restaurants!—but as good as venting would feel, I think it might be more effective to try to understand the source of our collective restaurant wine frustration and see if we can find a way to win the restaurant wine wars without resorting to bloodshed.

BOTTOM-LINE WINE

The cover of *Wine & the Bottom Line: A Training Manual* features a photo of a corkscrew halfway through its assigned task of extracting a cork from a bottle of white wine. Except that it's not a cork that's rising up through the neck—it is a rolled-up $100 bill. How to uncork restaurant wine profits—that's the message of this 1980 training manual published by the National Restaurant Association and written by Edmund Osterland, master sommelier.[3] Maybe it is my liberal arts training, but I like to get a historical perspective on contemporary problems so that I can appreciate what's changed (and try to figure out why) and what has stayed the same. And I like to look at things from the other side of the table, which in this case means taking the restaurant's perspective, not the outraged consumer's point of view, so I can't resist peering at today's restaurant wine wars through this thirty-five-year-old lens to see what the longer perspective might reveal.

Wine had a good run in the 1970s, the book begins, and the 1980s look to be even better. "In the decade of the 1980s, you will see changes in the consumer: a certain new affluence, an increased interest in international travel, and the development of a more individualistic lifestyle. Inevitably, the consumer's altered attitudes will have a direct influence on the products you will be selling—and, in particular, your wine selections."[4] That's twenty-twenty foresight, but the transformation wasn't necessarily as swift as Osterland guessed. Certainly, if you moved the date forward a few years, you would be talking about the world of restaurants and restaurant wine today.

"Better informed, and with well-defined tastes, these 'new' consumers of the 1980s will also be very definitely interested in GETTING VALUE FOR THEIR MONEY." The caps are in the original, which suggests that Osterland thought he needed to shout to get his readers' attention. "Because they will be vastly more knowledgeable about wine, they will know the approximate costs of varying wines . . . they will want to shop for the better values."[5] That paragraph has a contemporary ring to it, too. "For the first time you will experience customers who enter your restaurant and ask to see the wine list before the menu. . . . YOU MUST MAKE WINE A MAJOR PROFIT CENTER." OK, OK—you don't have to yell. But how?

There are only two things that are stopping restaurants from selling wine and making money, Osterland advises: supply and demand. That would mean the restaurants themselves and the wine-loving customers who frequent them. Restaurant staff, Osterland advised in 1980, are too often unfamiliar with the wine selections and poorly prepared to make recommendations. The wine selection itself is often poorly conceived and poorly presented, making the staff's job even harder. Restaurant patrons are not much better equipped. Lacking self-confidence when confronted with unfamiliar wines at high prices, they often balk when asked to pull the trigger on a wine order. Put the two groups together, and it seems like a miracle that any wine is sold in restaurants at all!

Osterland was probably exaggerating a bit to make his point. I am sure that there were many restaurants back in 1980 where well-informed, confident diners came together with well-priced and thoughtfully crafted wine lists and were guided by well-trained sommeliers. But there obviously were not enough of these matches made back then—that's why the National Restaurant Association thought it necessary to publish this training guide—and although things have changed a lot, there are probably not enough of them today, either. Hence the frustrating experiences that we love to hate.

THE MORE THINGS CHANGE

A lot has changed since Osterland's guide was published, but the problem persists. Restaurant wine is better now, I am sure, but there is plenty of room for improvement. The level of knowledge of and interest in wine has certainly risen in the thirty-plus years since the training manual was published. The United States has leap-frogged France to become the world's largest single wine market, for example. Magazines like *Wine Spectator, Wine Enthusiast, Wine & Spirits,* and *Food and Wine* are found on newsstands everywhere—in grocery stores, wine shops, drugstores, and convenience stores. And then there's the airport, which has become a big deal for wine, especially in duty-free shops at international hubs. Travelers find wine publications at airport kiosks, wine articles in the pages of the airline magazines that fill their seat pockets, wine bars in the terminals, and bottles of wine on the ubiquitous drinks cart. Wine, wine, wine, wine!

Wine clubs are erupting everywhere, too, both those created by particular wineries to sell their own products and ones that are sponsored by other enterprises as a way to leverage their customer lists to generate extra revenue. Who knew that the *Wall Street Journal* or *New York Times* would have wine clubs that offer carefully curated assortments of wines from around the world?

Differences in state regulations mean that while wine is not sold in supermarkets and grocery stores in every US state (the giant Eataly store in New York City ran afoul of state restrictions and had to replace its associated wine shop with a Nutella bar), you will find vast assortments of wine where such displays are legal, with hundreds and sometimes thousands of selections on offer.[6] I am tempted to say that wine has become more democratic, but, of course, it is more complicated than that, and wine has actually become both more democratic and more aristocratic at the same time. But even if it isn't a classless society, the world of wine is much bigger and broader than in years past, with more people drinking wine, learning about it, visiting wineries and tastings.

All good so far. But the world of wine is vast. The Masters of Wine that I know (and those studying for the qualification) all report that the process of becoming preeminent wine authorities is a humbling one, with each gain in knowledge and step towards completion revealing how much is left to learn. No wonder that wine drinkers lack confidence today, as Osterland said they did three decades ago.

The Wine and Spirit Education Trust (WSET), which sponsors wine classes and training around the world, released the results of a study of British wine drinkers in 2014 that shed light on the situation.[7] Although Londoners reported greater confidence in ordering wine than those outside the metropolitan area, fully 70 percent of respondents said that they resorted to "bluffing" at least some of the time when making wine choices, and they believed that their lack of knowledge made them less adventuresome than they would like to be. Osterland was right about wine consumers' growing appreciation for and interest in wine, but there's still a big gap between where diners are and where they feel they need to be in order to make confident restaurant wine choices.

Restaurants are giving more attention to wine today, too, yet there is still room to grow. Wine is an important potential profit center (that "bottom line" thing from the book title) and, as food costs and labor costs rise and postrecession diners remain cautious about their *own* bottom lines, value-added components of the meal like wine, designer cocktails, distinctive craft beers, and fancy desserts all receive a good deal of attention.

Restaurants that especially want to attract wine drinkers can signal their interest in many ways. They can host wine dinners, for example, where winemakers or distributors talk about their wines during a specially prepared multicourse meal. They can seek out recognition or certification, such as the *Wine Spectator* magazine's wine list awards. Restaurants apply to receive an Award of Excellence or be named to the more restrictive Best of Award of Excellence or Grand Award lists. In 2013, there were 3,800 restaurants worldwide that received this recognition. These awards and others like them do not necessarily guarantee excellent wine service or superior value, but they indicate an establishment that thinks seriously about its wine business and wants to attract diners who will appreciate the effort.

In my experience, staff training about wine has improved, but it is still a bit of a hit-or-miss proposition. We visited two Seattle restaurants located across the street from one another and owned by the same celebrity chef. In one, the waiter clearly knew a lot about the wine list and was pleased to help us pair our food with an interesting wine. At the other, the waiter knew nothing at all, except what he was told, which was to push certain dishes and certain wines. Sigh. Unsurprisingly, one experience was much more pleasant (and resulted in a better tip) than the other.

As Osterland noted, the merchandising of the wine is not an insignificant matter. Merchandising? There are many ways that a restaurant can attract appropriate attention to its wine list and help diners make choices. I have visited several restaurants that display bottles of wine (sometimes very large bottles!) near the entry, for example, to show diners their focus. And it is not uncommon for wine recommendations to be printed on the menu along with descriptions of each dish, encouraging diners to purchase wine by giving them a green light for a particular pairing. I singled out the restaurant chain Olive Garden for praise in *Wine Wars* because of their policy of giving wine away in small tastes to customers of legal drinking age (much as some ice cream and gelato stores will let visitors sample an icy treat before ordering). Having tasted the wine, Olive Garden customers were more likely to commit to a bottle or glass, which is one reason why Olive Garden sells more wine each year than any other restaurant group in the United States.

PRICE AND QUANTITY

If the source of the restaurant wine wars problem lies, as Osterland suggested years ago, in structural issues of both demand and supply, the actual battle seems focused on price and quantity. Diners complain that prices are generally too high and that the quantities, by which I really mean the selection of wines, is often either inappropriately large, creating confusion, or too narrow.

The selection problem is perhaps the most difficult, but alleged price gouging gets the most attention. There are tens of thousands of different wines made in the world, and choosing a few (or even a few hundred as I have seen at some wine-focused restaurants) is a daunting task. Winery and distributor representatives constantly approach restaurant wine buyers to pitch their wines. Which wines make the list depends a lot on the eatery's clients. If the customer base is curious or wine-savvy and the staff is enthusiastic and well-trained, then a range of quite specialized and possibly unfamiliar wines may be chosen to be hand-sold by staff to adventuresome customers. If, on the other hand, either staff or clientele are less sophisticated, then familiar names and varieties are more likely to be selected.

Wine & Spirits magazine polls restaurants about their wine sales each year to give us a glimpse into this world. The 2013 survey gathered information from 216 wine-friendly US restaurants that represent a slice of the market, but obviously not one that is representative of the whole industry (I don't see any Olive Gardens on the list of participants, for example).

Which wineries appear most frequently on the lists of these relatively elite restaurants? Number one in 2012 was Napa Valley's Cakebread Cellars (Cabernet, Chardonnay, and Sauvignon Blanc), which showed up in almost 12 percent of the responses. Duckhorn Vineyards, Stag's Leap Wine Cellars, Orin Smith, and Jordan round out the top five. These are not necessarily the top-five-selling restaurant wines, simply the ones that are most often found on wine lists of this type. The most frequently found imported wines were from Italy's Antinori (#6) and Santa Margherita (#17), Argentina's Catena (#12), and New Zealand's Cloudy Bay (#19). Significantly, the "concentration ratio" is very low—no short list of wineries dominates the league table. Wine lists tend to reflect the great variety of wine, as they should, even if it appears that most try to include familiar names.

What are the best-selling wines? *Wine & Spirits* asks restaurants to rank their top sellers, from 1 to 10, and then creates a composite ranking, which put Sonoma-Cutrer Chardonnay at the top with 81 points, followed, if I read the ratings correctly, by Jordan Cabernet with 75, Orin Smith Zinfandel with 69, and the Tuscan wines of Antinori with 65. The most popular "bargain" wines were Beringer White Zinfandel, Chateau Ste. Michelle Riesling, and Stella Umbrian Pinot Grigio. The Sonoma-Cutrer Chardonnay and Chateau Ste. Michelle Riesling were the most frequently mentioned wine-by-the-glass offerings.

Does this information surprise you? I guess it depends on what you expect and, of course, whether you frequent the sort of restaurants that participate in the *Wine & Spirits* poll. But you probably won't be surprised to learn about the price data that were reported. The Sonoma-Cutrer Chardonnay that topped the by-the-bottle and by-the glass lists sold for an average of $46 per bottle or $14 per glass. A quick Internet search found retail prices in the $20 to $25 range for the entry-level Sonoma Coast bottling. If the rule of thumb for restaurant wine-by-the-glass sales holds, which is that you charge per glass what you paid wholesale per bottle, then this wine was selling for an average of 200 percent of the typical retail price or 300 percent of the wholesale price.

Interestingly, the Chateau Ste. Michelle Riesling that came in as number two on the by-the-glass list sold for $11, which was not only more than its full-bottle wholesale price but actually more than the typical *retail* price, which I have seen as low as $5.99 and never higher than about $10. The average price for a restaurant bottle of this wine is reported by poll respondents to be $24. A nice wine—I drink it all the time at home—but at around 400 percent of wholesale price not a very nice restaurant wine value at the dining establishments that provided the data used in this poll. Perhaps the Chateau Ste. Michelle Riesling is a familiar "safety wine" on these by-the-glass lists and diners are taxed for their risk-aversion.

Edmund Osterland advised against such high markups in *Wine & the Bottom Line*. The better-informed consumers of 1980 wouldn't tolerate price abuse. "No longer can you mark up wine 400 percent; your customers will not accept that," he advises in the final chapter of the guide.[8] "Your pricing policy must be designed with your business *and* your customer in mind . . . your goal should be volume sales; attractive prices increase sales."

The key to Osterland's argument is something that economists call the "price elasticity of demand." If the demand for a product is unresponsive to price, or inelastic, as it would be for a necessity or something with few close substitutes, cutting price is not always wise for a business. Consumers simply pay less but purchase few extra bottles. Total revenue goes down. But if the demand is price elastic (as might be the case for a luxury good or one with many substitutes), lower price can be more than offset by higher sales volumes and total revenue increases. Osterland seems to think that the restaurant demand for wine is elastic, which would make sense if patrons saw it as a nonessential luxury or if they realized that there are many substitutes, such as drinking wine at home or at the restaurant across the street. While it may be true that the restaurant has a temporary monopoly on wine sales once you sit down to eat—not very feasible to search the Internet for a better deal at that point—Osterland looked to the long run and encouraged restaurants to drive their business with more affordable wines.

Is the *Wine & Spirits* data consistent with Osterland's viewpoint? You might not think so, since clearly some of those 400 percent markups are still around, but in another way they reflect the elasticity analysis pretty well. If someone is going to have just one glass of wine no matter what, then their demand is inelastic, and you might as well boost the price. But if they are treating themselves to an affordable luxury, then the price will be higher, but the markup can be less to encourage a return visit—or that much-desired order of a second bottle of wine.

THE CONVENTIONAL WISDOM IS WRONG

It sounds like the restaurant wars are still going on when it comes to wine—although there's been a lot of progress on the education front since 1980, there is also evidence that the system often fails, pitting unhappy restaurant owners and staff against disgruntled diners. What is to be done? I think it goes back to something Osterland said a few paragraphs ago about thinking about both sides of the restaurant wine experience and trying to work with your apparent opponents and not simply lash out against them.

According to WSET's survey of British wine drinkers, nearly 20 percent of wine drinkers bluff their way through the experience by pretending to study the wine list and then strategically ordering the second-cheapest wine that they find. You can't imagine how often I have heard this "second-cheapest" theory stated as fact. That's where the best value is, the story goes. The cheapest wine? That's just crap put there to trick you out of your money. And the more expensive bottles are even worse deals. The second-cheapest wine is really the best-value-in-a-decent-wine you will find—snap it up.

I am sure there are wine lists around the world where that second-cheapest wine is what you want to order, but I doubt that it holds up very well as a guideline, if only because if "everyone knows" that it is the wine you ought to choose, and if the restaurants are out to cheat you, which seems to be the premise behind the idea, then obviously restaurants *know* you are going to order it, and they will rig the wine list to make this the worst deal you can find. (Did that make sense?) If the game of Restaurant Wars is you versus the house, then a strategy like this is bound to fail. Besides, as we learned from a quick look at the *Wine & Spirits* survey, sometimes less-expensive wines actually have higher-percentage markups than costlier wines.

When it comes to the second-cheapest rule, it is important to remember the lessons from earlier chapters in this book. We seem to be programmed to think about wine in terms of money and to jump to unjustified conclusions. We must fight the urge to think that price is a reliable guide to quality.

Another rule of thumb to avoid concerns wine by the glass. "Never buy wine by the glass, this principle holds, the wines are old and tired and the prices are too high. Don't fall for the wine-by-the glass trap." There is something to be said for the first part of this statement. In restaurants where by-the-glass bottles are simply recorked and where such sales are slow, the wines may well deteriorate in the time between the first glass pour and the last (or when the bottle is dumped out because it has lost too much quality). It is best to order glasses of wine in restaurants where a lot of other people do the same, because this promises faster turnover and fresher wine. Some restaurants have invested in wine-preservation systems that help assure that the first and last glass poured from a bottle have equal quality. Fleming's Prime Steakhouse & Wine Bar, a US restaurant chain, offers a hundred wines by the glass, for example, a feat that would be insane without a good preservation system and a steady turnover of wines. In fact, Fleming's makes this an important part of their marketing effort, encouraging wine lovers to visit, have a glass or two, and return again and again. Very clever.

Technological change is actually making wine by the glass a better deal for both diners and the restaurants themselves because of the rise of keg-wine sales. Keg wines come in sealed stainless-steel containers that typically hold about 20 liters of wine—equivalent to 26 standard bottles. Inert gas keeps the wine fresh as it is served. Lower cost—which at least sometimes is passed along in lower prices—less waste, fresher wine. Keg wine is not the answer to all the Restaurant Wars' wine problems, but it is a step in the right direction.

So the second-cheapest wine is not always the best choice, and by-the-glass wines aren't always bad deals. Two treasured rules shot down in flames. Is there any surefire rule for wine in restaurants? I think that it is useful for diners to think about what I have already said in this book, for restaurants to pay attention to Osterland's decades-old advice, and for all of us to heed the lessons of *Top Chef*'s Restaurant Wars competitions, too.

Chapter 3 of this book stressed the fact that while it might be impossible for most wine enthusiasts to know all about the world of wine, perhaps they should look inward instead and follow the classic advice "know thyself." An understanding of what types of wines you most enjoy and what your wine-price comfort zone is can go a long way toward making the restaurant wine experience more successful. This is especially true if restaurants take Osterland's advice and train their staffs about the wines they serve and present them effectively so that diners will have confidence ordering them and will want to return in the future. A diner who knows herself and the waiter or sommelier who understands the wine list and knows how to listen make a great team that both satisfies the client and builds the bottom line.

Some of my best restaurant wine experiences have come when I've been able to tell the waiter what we want to eat, what kinds of wines we like, and how much we would like to pay. "What do you recommend?" A knowledge-able and well-trained waiter will rise to this challenge just about every time. Working together—rather than trying to throw each other under the bus—they can win the Restaurant Wars competition. If they don't work together (or if their teamwork is sabotaged by sky-high prices)? Expect unhappy customers to head for that restaurant across the street. Or at least that's what happens on *Top Chef.*

Chapter 12

Follow the Money

October. This is one of the peculiarly dangerous months to speculate in
stocks. The others are July, January, September, April, November, May,
March, June, December, August, and February.

—*Mark Twain, Pudd'nhead Wilson (1894)*

I wonder what Mark Twain would say about speculating in *wine* in October,
May, or any other month? I expect he would be suspicious of the idea. Twain
was a great author but a lousy investor. His cautious attitude toward money
as expressed here was based upon his own disastrous financial experiences (he
declared bankruptcy at age fifty-eight—in the very year of this quote!). I am
cautious, too, when it comes to money and suspicious of sure-thing investment propositions especially, as you will see in this chapter, when it comes to
investing in wine.

WHAT TIME IS IT?

I was reminded of the Twain quote one morning a few years ago when I
opened the *New York Times* "Special Section on Wealth & Personal Finance."
The cover featured a half-page color image of an exploding cherry pie (or
maybe it's strawberry—hard to tell). I am not really sure what it meant. But
the theme of the special section was pretty clear—time to consider alternative
investments and investment strategies—a promising idea given the dismal

conventional investment climate then prevailing. And on page 4, I found the article that got me thinking about Mr. Twain's investment advice: "Investing in Wine: Now May Be the Time."[1] "It's a great time to buy wine, the best time in a decade," according to Charles Curtis, who was then head of Christie's auction house North American wine department. "People we've never heard of are jumping into the market, taking advantage of the lull to get into collecting, now that they have access."

The idea back in 2009 when the article was written was that fine-wine prices had been falling, so this was an opportunity to buy in at the market bottom. The prices of investment-grade wines did rise, so the advice was not without merit, but then they fell again the way that investment valuations sometimes do, and they are sliding lower as this is written. Is this once again a good time to invest?

I am naturally a bit suspicious of buying advice given by people with an interest in the sales. They always seem to think that *right now* is the time to buy. Rising prices? Buy now because they can only go higher. Falling prices? Buy now before they rise again. I'm exaggerating to be sure, but sometimes it reminds me of that old Paul Masson wine television commercial, which featured the actor Orson Welles proclaiming, "We will sell no wine before it's time." What time is it, one joker asked? It's time!

INVESTING IN FINE WINE

Fine wine is often categorized as an alternative investment class by those in the know, which puts wine in a category that includes collectible art, jewelry and watches, precious metals, and vintage automobiles, which are "alternatives" to the usual financial investments, such as stocks and bonds. Why would you invest in (as opposed to collect or purchase to drink) fine wine? Presumably because you think its investment return will exceed the alternatives or because its pattern of rises and falls is sufficiently different from other investments to represent a valid way to diversify your portfolio.

How you see wine investing depends upon how you look at it. Compared with other alternative investments, such as fine art and rare automobiles, the fine-wine investment market is very well organized. In addition to periodic auctions where all these products are bought and sold, for example, the fine-wine market has developed a number of sophisticated electronic "trading platforms" (something like the electronic stock exchange trading floors), where wines can be bought and sold with high transparency and relatively low transactions costs. The most noteworthy of these trading platforms is called the Liv-ex exchange, which publishes a number of well-publicized wine-price indices, much in the spirit of the Dow Jones, Russell, and London's FTSE stock listings.

The thing about investing is this—if you are going to put your money into an investment, you need to know that you can get it out when you want or need to. This is called liquidity, and if an asset isn't very liquid—that is, if it cannot easily and cheaply be converted into cash—that adds an additional element of risk to the deal, and you will want to earn an appropriately higher return as compensation. Ironically, wine—perhaps the most liquid asset possible, in a physical sense—is not the world's most liquid investment asset. Wine investments look to me to be more liquid than art and autos, for example, but less liquid compared with conventional investments like stocks and bonds. US Treasury securities are arguably the most liquid investments on earth—the market for them sees incredible buy and sell flows every day—which compensates for the fact that their returns are relatively low.

The problem with fine-wine investment so far—and I think that this is changing—is that most of the action has been in a very small number of particular assets, mainly the famous names from Bordeaux. This makes the wine investment market a bit like the stock exchange in one of those emerging-market countries where the stocks of one or two companies dominate the action. Hard to diversify your portfolio under these circumstances and hard to assure liquidity since bandwagon effects are possible where everyone wants to surge in or to escape from their investments at the same time. This doesn't always happen, of course, it is just more likely in narrow, thin markets where diversification is difficult compared with broad (lots of different assets) and deep (lots of traders and trading) markets.

For many years, waves of wine investors put their chips on the famous Bordeaux reds and rode out the booms and busts that resulted. American investors replaced European ones and then Chinese investors stepped in when Americans backed off. Now it seems that the Chinese might have all the Bordeaux that they think they need, too, and the focus has shifted to other wines, which usefully broadens the market and perhaps even signals the start of a new era when people like me will be a little less suspicious of wine-investment pitches. Rare Champagnes, top red Burgundies, the most sought-after Super Tuscans, and a smattering of famous wines from California, Australia, and Spain—these new elements of the wine market aren't enough to transform the investment environment for wine, but they are a step in the right direction.

THE *EN PRIMEUR* CIRCUS

The decline in interest (among investors at least) in the famous wines of Bordeaux became so severe in 2014 that it threatened that region's peculiar institution, the *en primeur* circus. The top Bordeaux winemakers actually sell their wines *before* their time, in a clear violation of the Paul Masson rule. The wines are only released—bottled, blended, barrel-aged, and ready to go—two or three years after the grapes are harvested. But the wines are sold just a few months after vintage, while still young, in the barrel, in the process of developing, and before a final blend of grape varieties has been made (Bordeaux wines are almost always blends, but rival Burgundy wines are a single grape variety). Buyers pay now based on critics' reviews and their own analysis without being perfectly certain what the market conditions will be when the wines are finally released to them or even what the wines themselves will be.

I call it the *en primeur* circus not because there are tigers and elephants involved (as entertaining as that would be) but rather because of the crush of critics, wine writers, and wine traders who descend on Bordeaux each spring to try to assess the wines and read the market tea leaves. Sometimes they make me think of those little circus cars that unexpectedly disgorge two or three dozen brightly dressed clowns. What a riot! You get the gag, I hope. But there are more than a few chuckles at stake in Bordeaux.

If this "buy the wine before it's time" system sounds more like speculation than investment to you, I tend to agree, but not everyone sees it that way. For a number of years it seemed as if "investing" in top-flight Bordeaux wines *en primeur* was one of the true sure things in the money and wine game. You paid your money now, and in two years or so the wines would appear and magically be selling on the open market for more than you paid. You could almost count on making a profit when the wines were delivered and maybe even cashing out earlier by simply selling on your *en primeur* rights to a willing buyer. Pretty sweet!

My gut feeling is that *en primeur* changed for good a few years ago, and Liv-ex data released in late 2013 bears this out. People tend to measure the success of an *en primeur* campaign by their ability to profit from it, and the profits in the past were often very large and generously distributed down the supply chain. I think there was an "invisible handshake" agreement among market participants. Everyone in the supply chain left a bit of "meat-on-the-bone" profit for the next person to take so that the whole system—with its substantial collective benefits—was safe and secure. The seemingly sure prospect of quick profit greased the wheels of commerce on Place de Bordeaux.

But then two things happened. The first, I would argue, was a simple realization that perhaps it wasn't really necessary for the châteaux to leave so much profit for others. Perhaps the wines would sell at higher prices with more of the scarcity rents accruing to the producers and fewer profits left for others to enjoy. The Liv-ex data suggest that this process probably gained traction around the 2005 vintage, when returns to *en primeur* buyers suddenly plunged. The invisible handshake that seemed to guarantee profits for one and all suddenly disappeared.

Then came the global financial crisis, which introduced additional risk to the *en primeur* equation. Fine wine, like other investments, is necessarily affected by economic risk. A lot can go wrong with any financial investment, and regulations require disclosure in full, gory detail. The *Oxford Companion to Wine*'s article on *en primeur* might be seen as a very simple prospectus for this sort of investment, and it describes the nature of risk on this market very well. Nice profits when things are rolling along, it says, but look out when a recession hits. Those seemingly guaranteed returns start to evaporate and counterparty risk (the risk that someone in the supply chain who owes you something—your promised money, your promised wine—can't honor the obligation) becomes a concern.

The financial crisis intensified the scramble for profits up and down the supply chain. The combination of the continuing recession, the increase in risk, and the end of the invisible handshake (plus China's fading interest) made the good times of the past a distant memory. A study released by Liv-ex showed how dramatic and sudden the shift has been. Eight out of ten *en primeur* markets produced strong profits between 1995 and 2005, sometimes with profits of 50 percent or more for buyers who "flipped" their early purchases. The game changed starting with 2006, however, with *en primeur* losses for every vintage except 2008.[2]

As I wrote the first draft of this chapter in early 2014, there seemed to be little enthusiasm for the *en primeur* market. In part, this was because of the results of the last two years' campaigns, which some declared disastrous, with overpriced wines, unwanted inventory accumulations, and rivers of red ink. Many buyers, it is said, were tired of the game and turned their attention elsewhere. And then there was the depressing prospect of the weather-plagued 2013 vintage itself. Robert Joseph and some others wondered if the wines would be good enough to carry the weight of expectations. Perhaps the great châteaux would be wise to produce no *grand vin* wines this year rather than releasing second-rate and possibly overpriced ones? I can almost hear the sighs of relief that might greet such a decision, which would give everyone a chance to reset and reload, drawing down inventories and building up demand.

No *grands vins*? No *en primeur* campaign? While some might prefer taking a pass on *en primeur* in another disastrous year, many others depend on the annual rite and the revenues it generates. It is not clear that everyone who plays the *en primeur* game can afford to take a year off. Will things return to what used to pass for normal in future years or does this crisis herald a long-term shift? Wait and see—we make no wine investment predictions before their time!

RED, WHITE, PINK, AND BLACK (GOLD) WINES

Here's a question that few conventional investors will ever have to confront: Which do you prefer, Great Bordeaux or bulk crude oil? For drinking there is no choice—red wine trumps black gold (even light sweet crude). No doubt about it. But how about if you look at the choice from an *investment* perspective? The surprising answer is that it makes little difference. The prices of fine wine and crude oil have been highly correlated in recent years. Or at least that is the conclusion of two economists at the International Monetary Fund (IMF), Serhan Cevik and Tahsin Saadi Sedik, as reported in their 2011 paper

"A Barrel of Oil or a Bottle of Wine: How Do Global Growth Dynamics Affect Commodity Markets?"[3]

According to the IMF study, price indices for crude oil and investment-grade wine are highly correlated. Wine follows the twists and turns of oil prices, but it is somewhat less volatile in terms of peaks and troughs. The conclusions are more or less the same if real (inflation-adjusted) data are used instead of nominal measures. Who would have guessed? As this is being written, the prices of both investment-quality wine and crude oil are at lows not seen for many years.

What do oil and fine wine have in common? Darn little, from the drinking standpoint, but quite a lot in terms of supply and demand. Both commodities have relatively inelastic supplies (for very different reasons, as you may imagine), according to the study authors, so that changes in demand account for the majority of price movements. The authors find that the same macroeconomic factors that push up the global demand for oil are associated with rising auction prices for the fine wines in the Liv-ex index. Certainly, in recent years it must be true that China's fast growth and recent slowdown hit the relatively narrow investment-wine market and the much broader global commodities markets in the same way, albeit for different specific reasons. As I write this, the price of crude oil is in a slump and so are the prices of investment-quality Bordeaux vintages.

So what? The study tells us a number of interesting things. First, it indicates that economists at the IMF aren't afraid to think outside the box—a good thing, I suppose, since they are part of the glue that holds the global financial system together (hey, Mr. Euro, I'm talkin' 'bout you!). Wine and oil? What a crazy idea. Second, it shows that adding wine to an investment portfolio does not necessarily usefully diversify it if oil is also in the mix. You might not have guessed this correlation, but there it is. Always good to do research and not rely entirely upon common sense or intuition.

Finally, the authors note an important shift in the global economic center of gravity. Whereas only a few years ago the changes in both oil and wine prices would have been explained by US and Western European economic variables, now the emerging markets have the most clout. The driving forces of world commodity markets have new postal codes. You don't need to read tea leaves to get the new address—wine and oil both point the way!

MONEY AND WINE: A COMPLICATED TRANSFORMATION

Money and wine are closely tied, but not by a simple knot. It is pretty easy to convert money into wine, for example. In fact, it may be a little *too* easy to do this. Some of my friends report that the whole "money into wine" thing has gotten way out of hand for them, and they worry whenever they walk into a wine shop or open an e-mail from a flash wine sales site. You probably know the problem from personal experience if your cellar has grown bigger than your bank account. It is harder to convert wine into money, especially if you are in the wine business.

Maybe I am gun-shy when it comes to wine investing because I have spent so much of my professional career studying economic crises. I am ever mindful of the words of Walter Bagehot, the first editor of the *Economist* newspaper, who described the way that financial bubbles gathered pace by attracting the attention of hitherto uninvolved investors, such as authors, rectors, and grandmothers. "At intervals . . . the money from these people—the blind capital, as we call it, of the country—is particularly craving; it seeks out for someone to devour it, and there is a 'plethora'; it finds some one, and there is 'speculation'; it is devoured, and there is 'panic.'"[4] Blind capital . . . devoured. Not an image to give a newbie investor much comfort. But novice investors in fine wine probably don't read much nineteenth-century political economy— maybe they should.

So it is not surprising that I am very cautious when it comes to the fine-wine investment business. But then I'm not really a wine investor—I buy wine to drink and enjoy. I have a couple of "collectible" bottles stashed away for special occasions (I've promised myself not to drink them before their time), but I don't have any plans to sell any of these bottles for a profit, which, of course, is what an investor would want to do. In my reading, I find the terms "wine investor" and "wine collector" often used as synonyms, but I'm not sure they should be. A wine collector buys what he or she wants to own (and, presumably, drink). It's a personal thing. A wine investor *should* buy what *other people* will want to own, which might have nothing to do with personal taste.

I have known only a few real wine investors but lots of wine collectors who justify at least some of their purchases as investments, but who don't manage them as they would a real investment. For some of them, at least, the excuse that fine wine is an investment is really a cover story, and the underlying truth that it hides is the passion to have and to hold rare wines. Sometimes the passion even pays but, as we will now learn, sometimes it doesn't.

WINE CRIME DOESN'T ALWAYS PAY

This chapter has been fairly serious, as any discussion of money should be, but let me bring it to a close on a lighter note. What happens when you combine two familiar sayings: "crime doesn't pay" and "the best way to make a small fortune in wine is to start with a big one?" You would think that it would add up to the conclusion that if crime doesn't pay, then wine crime *really* doesn't pay. But that may not be true. How else can we explain the recent fine-wine crime wave?

When they asked the legendary criminal Willie Sutton why he robbed banks, he replied, "Because that's where the money is." There is money in wine, too, so maybe it is not surprising that criminals are part of the wine scene, and the wine-investor equivalent of a bank is a secured, temperature-controlled wine-storage warehouse of the type that can be found in many big cities. As wine investment has accelerated, the value of the holdings in these air-conditioned vaults has also grown.

Wine theft gets less public notice than bank robbery or even other forms of wine crime. Wine fraud, much like art fraud, seems to be almost inevitable when passionate investors and collectors seeking rare artistic gems meet nefarious individuals who are willing to feed their passion and devour their capital, and several notorious cases of fake wine have hit the headlines in recent years (I wrote about them in *Extreme Wine*). The Great Seattle Thanksgiving Day wine heist was a grittier affair but perhaps equally interesting to wine-crime buffs. I've been trying to piece together what happened from published reports and private sources. The more I learn about it the more this crime reminds me of something from a television show—*CSI* or *Mission Impossible* (or possibly *Monty Python's Flying Circus*)!

Two "common thieves" (plumbers by trade, according to the Seattle police) broke into the wine-storage facility operated by Esquin wine merchants in the SoDo neighborhood.[5] They ransacked 15 of the 450 private storage lockers in the climate-controlled facility and made off with more than 200 cases of wine, valued in excess of $600,000. If you are doing the math, that's an average of more than $3,000 per case or more than $250 per bottle. I'm guessing that no Two Buck Chuck was taken!

The break-in was ingenious—the perpetrators apparently cut a hole through a wall and brought the wine out case by case. Police report that the crooks spent thirteen hours selecting their wines and then driving the loot to another warehouse less than a mile away. Their getaway SUV had limited capacity, so they had to make nine round-trips. Although they blacked out all the security cameras that they could, apparently this was not completely successful, and some images of the crooks and their SUV's license plate were captured.

You would think that "common thieves" would not be terribly discriminating wine shoppers—after all, I suspect that most of the bottles and cases at this storage facility were of considerable value. Why not just smash and grab? But that's not what happened. The two bad guys apparently worked from some sort of shopping list, taking specific wines and vintages and leaving the rest. I'm told that the only Washington State wines taken were Quilceda Creek and Corliss, for example. Leonetti and Andrew Will? Apparently not up to the discerning crooks' standards! I understand that wine was not just stolen, but it also moved around and mixed up during the extended shopping spree, and a few of the victims apparently had to sort out which wines were theirs, which belonged to someone else, and which bottles had gone missing.

A good, old-fashioned paper trail of evidence helped solve the crime, and it now opens the door to solving other possible heists. The first criminal captured had apparently kept receipts from a home improvement store—great idea in case you need to return an item!—and police used the day/time information on the receipts to access security-camera footage showing the suspect and his accomplice buying the hardware used in the criminal act. According to the *Seattle Times*, a second paper trail opens the door to an earlier wine theft. "A shipping label found in Harris' wine-storage locker led detectives to a San Francisco wine consultant, who told police he purchased $100,000 of wine from Harris and another man in April or May, charging papers say. Through an online search, Detective Don Jones determined there had been a large wine theft in the Bay Area in March, the papers say."[6]

Seattle's KOMO news reported another *Mission Impossible*–style detail about the carefully plotted plan to crack the wine storage facility. "New details from the charging documents filed Monday reveal police found a journal labeled

'The Plan' in Harris' SUV. The journal reportedly included a step-by-step guide to the crime, a list of needed equipment, steps to destroy any evidence, steps to ship the wine and how to leave the country."[7] Seattle police also discovered a book called *Thinking about Crime* and a print-out of documents titled "How to Commit the Perfect Crime" and "Is It Accidental Fire or Arson?" Where does the arson come in? The thieves planned to cover their tracks in the most comprehensive possible way. They cut gas lines and expected the building to blow up. Good fortune prevented any loss of life, and good police work captured the criminals. Some of the victims are more upset about the idea of the flaming cover-up plan, with its potentially tragic consequences, than about the actual robbery.

So case closed for now—the thieves in custody and a good chance that most of the wine (minus one empty Champagne bottle) has been recovered. But are these two common thieves the whole story? Or is there a criminal mastermind still at large making up a shopping list for clients too smart to buy fakes but maybe not too smart to avoid stolen goods? Good question!

So welcome to the new era of wine, taste, and money, where the questions a fine-wine enthusiast needs to ask now range from red or white and Burgundy or Bordeaux all the way to real or fake, stolen or legit?

Should you invest in fine wine? Despite my obvious caution, I will say that alternative investment is not a crazy idea and that some small fortunes have been made by those with good timing and a good sense of the shifting market demand. But that "know thyself" advice from earlier in the book applies: Are you an investor who buys to resell at a profit, or a collector who longs to have and to hold (and drink) as long as you both shall live?

Chapter 13

Invisible Cities, Imaginary Wines

Kublai Khan is old and tired and his empire is vast and fraying at the edges. It is impossible for him personally to know his great domain, so he studies his atlas and sends emissaries to be his eyes and ears and bring back reports. His favorite eye-witness correspondent is Marco Polo, with whom he sits for days on end in the palace garden, turning gestures and then words into vivid images of otherwise unseen cities via the advanced technology of the human imagination.

Are the stories and the cities they represent truth or fiction? It is impossible for Kublai Khan to know for sure since they cannot easily be verified. Some of the tales are fantastic and understandably raise doubts. But they all seem to contain an ephemeral kernel of truth, which makes the invisible cities important even if they are only figments of the imagination.

In any case, Marco Polo advises, the truth is in the hearing, not the telling, since each listener (or reader, I suppose) will shape the words to reflect their own experiences, anxieties, and desires. The same accounts, he advises Kublai, will produce entirely different images when he eventually tells them again back home in Venice.

INVISIBLE CITIES, INVISIBLE WINES

Do you recognize this story? It is from one of my favorite books, Italo Calvino's *Invisible Cities*.[1] This is a book that I have read and reread perhaps ten times, with those bits of truth always just beyond my reach (perhaps this is why Kublai Khan spends so much time with Marco Polo). It is a great book, but what does it have to do with wine?

I was inspired to dig out my copy of *Invisible Cities* by a recent column by *New York Times* wine critic Eric Asimov called "Why Can't You Find That Wine?"[2] Asimov uses the article to respond to readers who are frustrated that the fabulous wines he often praises turn out to be nearly impossible for them to actually experience. No amount of money, it seems, can secure for them the taste of these wines. Asimov writes,

> Often plaintive and occasionally hostile, the missives arrive regularly by email, snail mail and phone: "You have an uncanny ability to discuss wines that are difficult if not impossible to find," one California reader wrote in June. And this from a reader in New York: "Once again, I have wasted more than a half-hour trying (in vain) to find where in New York City to buy wines mentioned in your column."

Asimov is sympathetic to his readers' frustration and explains how the almost hopelessly fragmented US wine market (a lasting legacy of Prohibition) makes it nearly impossible to talk about important wines if you limit your list to only those that can be found in all the nation's many marketplaces. He usefully provides hints and strategies for consumers to use to track down special wines:

> "My goal is to explore what I think makes wine so thrilling," Asimov writes. "I'm seeking wines that inspire, with stories to tell and mysteries, perhaps, to conceal. Sometimes deliciousness is enough. But often, the flavors and aromas are only part of what a wine conveys. It's the rest of the message that's so fascinating. Part of the joy is for consumers to take part in this journey and make up their own minds. It hurts when they cannot."

Many of the wines that Asimov finds inspiring are produced or imported in tiny quantities with very limited distribution. The wines are real, but for most of Asimov's readers they might as well be imaginary since their only chance to experience them is to imagine them, much as Kublai Kahn imagined Marco Polo's cities.

THE EMPIRE OF IMAGINARY WINES

"I fervently wish all drinkers could find what they want. I sympathize with those who can't," Asimov writes. "But the simple solution—choosing only wines that are easy to find—is worse than the problem." That's because Asimov sees his mission not just to report but to elevate and inspire—to excite our imaginations and to draw attention to those who somehow through their winemaking are able to bring us a bit closer to an ephemeral kernel of truth.

Those are my words, not his, but you get the idea. And do you see how Asimov and Marco Polo are connected? They both tell us stories about a world too vast for us to ever really know. There are, I am told, about 80,000 different wines for sale in the United States today—far too many for any of us to know and appreciate, even if they were all available to us in one easy-to-shop aisle, which of course they are not. They are a bit like Kublai Kahn's vast empire (and we are a bit like him, I suppose).

Eighty thousand wines? That seems like a lot, but there are probably even more. *Wine Business Monthly* reports that there are about eight thousand wineries in North America, and if each produced just five different wines, that would account for half the total. Could the rest of the world with its many thousands of wineries supply the rest? My goodness, yes.

But can you find them to purchase? Check the Internet, which is increasingly seen as a potential solution to the imaginary wine problem within the United States, especially if regulations on interstate wine shipments are ever liberalized. But finding physical bottles of wine as opposed to virtual sales vectors is always going to be a problem because there is no real national wine market, only the fifty separate state wine-regulatory regimes (plus D.C.), which require local distribution and control. Small-production wineries (or international producers with small import footprints) long ago learned that taking on the whole country is prohibitively expensive. Better to have limited visibility by strategically focusing on a few markets.

New York, where Asimov is based, would be on almost everyone's short list of targets, along with Florida, Texas, California, and probably Illinois. There are other very good markets, depending on origin and type of wine (the East Coast leans toward Europe, the West Coast more toward New World wines), but if your scale is small, you need to focus. And often the specific target of those who make the very interesting wines that Asimov loves to ponder are restaurants, not retail wine shops. Special wines benefit from the "hand-selling" by trained sommeliers who can tell a wine's story and match it with food.

The result? Finding a specific small-lot wine (and some with thousands of cases in distribution) even in New York can be a frantic treasure hunt experience. Finding the wines in a state outside of the target market bull's-eye can be like looking for a needle in a haystack, even with the Internet's help.[3] (One of my *Wine Economist* readers suggests that wine reviews include importer or distributor names and contact details—a very useful idea!)

IMAGINARY WINE: A NEW WINE GENRE?

So we truly are in Kublai Khan's position, aren't we? The difference, I suppose, is that unlike him we are not satisfied with a glimpse of the truth to inspire us—we want to see the invisible cities and to taste the invisible wines, and we won't be satisfied until we do.

I am sure that Asimov is right—it is probably best for him to tell us about inspiring wines even if we can never know them, since the tales of exotic pleasures may inspire us even if they also frustrate us. (There is a place, however, for news and reviews of the visible wines, too, don't you think?) But perhaps we need to take the next step. Asimov's wines are real, but if we cannot taste them ourselves, wouldn't inspiring stories about fictional wines be just as good—or maybe even better?

I guess what I am asking is if there is a place in the wine world for fantastically fictional descriptions of imaginary wines that would make us rethink money, taste, and wine the way that Marco Polo's stories made Kublai Khan rethink his (and our) world? We could never taste the wines, but perhaps they might still elevate and inspire.

Perhaps there is no other way to reconcile money, taste, and wine in the extreme case where money and taste can't have the wine. A radical thought? No, just a practical solution. I remember from my university mathematics classes that when a certain class of problem could not be solved with real numbers, some mathematicians had the great idea to invent imaginary numbers. And bingo! Problem solved. I wonder if imaginary wines could have the same impact?

UNCOOKED KOSHER WINE

If you were Marco Polo describing an imaginary wine to Kublai Kahn, what would you say? One of my readers responded with a tasting note he found on the Web: "The wine has the aroma of baby's breath and the flavor of mother's milk."[4] Provocative. Evocative. Sounds exactly like something Marco Polo would say to Kublai Kahn. I had to find out more.

The wine in question is called Tiferet and is produced by Summerhill Pyramid Winery in scenic Kelowna, British Columbia, Canada. (As I explained in *Extreme Wine*, perhaps unexpectedly, Canada has two regions where excellent wine is produced—Ontario and the Okanagan region of British Columbia.) The wine, made from Merlot, Cabernet Sauvignon, and Cabernet Franc and aged in 100 percent new American and French oak, is said to be Canada's first "uncooked" kosher wine and sells for the princely sum of $100 per bottle. I have not tasted it, and given that only about 1,200 numbered bottles were made (and shipping wine to the United States from Canada is even more difficult than shipping within that country), perhaps I never will. So maybe the baby's breath, mother's milk description provided by the winemaker will have to suffice, and that's fine, but I am curious. My memory of the taste of mother's milk is not very fresh, but the Merlot-based wines that I have sampled in the past have not tasted like milk of any kind.

I am sure that the wine really exists, but its story is so fantastic that you really couldn't make it up. The kosher wine aspect is conventional if still unusual. Sampling a selection of kosher wines with his friend Rabbi Shmuly Hecht, the winery's CEO, Ezra Cipes, was disappointed and accused the rabbi of not knowing what real quality wine was like. He blamed the heating process generally used to make kosher wines for the lack of quality and set out to make a quality "uncooked" wine. The rabbi performed all of the winemaking and bottling functions himself (he even applied the wax seal over the cork), and the end result was that it received the *hechsher* ("kosher approval") of Ottawa Vaad Hakashrut (the nearest certifying agency).

Summerhill Pyramid Winery's conventional wines win awards, and the winery itself is a popular visitor stop. It is easy to spot because of the pyramid—yes, a real pyramid that is "second only to the Great Pyramid of Egypt for alignment and precision," according to the website. It was built as part of an ongoing experiment to determine if cosmic forces can affect wine as it develops (an idea that will be familiar to anyone who has stored razor blades in a tiny cardboard pyramid to prolong their sharp lives). Like biodynamic farming, which is also practiced here, there is a bit of the voodoo feeling to this, but if the wines are very good, who am I to criticize? And if they taste like mother's milk, I must applaud!

RIDICULOUS EXTREMES: PRESCRIPTION WINE

Sometimes people say that something is "too good to be true," but I suppose the mother's milk of the uncooked kosher wine is actually too good to be fiction. But it is the fictional wines, the ones that can only exist in my imagination, that I am interested in now. But how to think about them? I found my inspiration in an unlikely source, the works of the Italian author and professor Umberto Eco. Not his famous novels like *The Name of the Rose* and not his scholarly essays on semiotics. No, instead I looked to the short columns that he used to write for Italian newspapers, which were collected under the title *How to Travel with a Salmon and Other Essays*.[5] I have read and reread this slim volume almost as many times over the years as Calvino's *Invisible Cities*.

Eco's method, I observe in these essays, is to create some sort of organization or taxonomy and then press on to whatever ridiculous extreme results—ridiculous in a good way in this case because the essays are meant to satirize, amuse, and inform. With this in mind, I tried to imagine wines that don't yet (to my knowledge) exist.

Wines tend to be defined by place of origin (Burgundy, Bordeaux) or grape variety (Merlot, Pinot Noir), but less so by specific site of sale or consumption. So perhaps this is a first imaginary wine genre we can explore. Wine is increasingly sold not just in restaurants, supermarkets, or specialist shops but everywhere. Indeed, it is said that during the Great Recession in the United States a particularly popular Australian wine brand (you can probably guess the color of its "tail") shifted its sales emphasis from supermarkets to pharmacies and drugstores, which were in any case trying to expand their product lines beyond the traditional lotions, potions, and pills.

If someone made a wine specifically for drugstores, what would it be?[6] It seems like there would be two distinct types. Not red versus white or still versus sparkling, but prescription versus over-the-counter (OTC). What would be the difference? Could be based purely on alcoholic strength, I suppose, but where's the fun in that? No, I propose that the OTC wines be less-sophisticated versions of the bottle behind the glass booth, which you can get only with an illegible note from a board-certified sommelier who can attest to your ability to enjoy and appreciate fine wine. Perhaps the pharmacists themselves can be trained in wine appreciation, too, so that they can recommend particular wines with confidence.

I like this scheme (and I imagine that some form of it will actually appear, since wine sales have high margins), but I admit that it doesn't fully exploit the pharmacy's potential as a specialized wine venue. Health and beauty—these are the traditional stock-in-trade of ye olde chemist's shoppe, so perhaps wines can be blended to make the consumer particularly beautiful or unusually healthful. Some sort of wine bath gel, perhaps? The current boom in so-called natural wines (made without sulfur dioxide or other standard additives) could be exploited by placing some of them in the naturopathic medicine aisle, for example. And red wines, which are famously associated with the French Wine Paradox, could be arrayed alongside medications designed to reduce cholesterol counts.

My final suggestion is a bit technical but not, I hope, uninteresting. There is a certain wine feature (to some) and wine flaw (to others) that is called *Brettanomyces*. "Brett," as it is called in the trade, is a rogue yeast that, in small quantities, produces the earthiness or "barnyard" aromas that some wine drinkers love. In slightly larger amounts, the smell is more like a Band-Aid strip. Exciting to some, but a turnoff to others; I would, of course, put these wines among the medical bandages and ointments.

CHÂTEAU PETROL PÉTRUS

In their quest to sell wine to everyone everywhere, wine merchants have also moved to petrol stations (service stations or gas stations here in the United States). Indeed, at least one local petrol station, owned by a wine lover, sells not just wine but *fine* wine and was the subject of a certain amount of unfair humor on a national late-night television show. Fine wine at a gas station? Ridiculous! But then again, why not? BMW owners buy gas, too, don't they? Why shouldn't the Château Petrol on the corner sell Château Pétrus? No reason, I say!

But what particular wine would make the most sense for buyers at petrol stations? Let me skip my proposal for leaded and unleaded wine (some wines—Cabernet Franc among them—are thought to sometimes display the aroma of pencil lead). That's more of a play on words than an actual feature of the wines. "Petrol," on the other hand, is an accepted wine descriptor, and it is a feature sometimes found in some Riesling wines. Like Brett, it is loved by some and loathed by others—I quite like these kind of smells and am not alone. A friend or ours once swooned over a particular Chilean Cabernet that she said reminded her of walking into her father's garage after he had changed the car's oil.

Petrol wines seem like a particularly good idea to me, but I can see the need for other wines, if only to fill the otherwise quite bare shelves. One approach would be to match Château Petrol wines to the traditional petrol-station food items, such as chili dogs here in the United States and pork or steak and kidney pies in much of the rest of the world. (The BP New Zealand website actually lists a selection of "gourmet pies" on offer, including Thai Chicken and Vegetarian Deluxe, but I don't know why a health-conscious vegetarian would eat a petrol station pie of any sort.) I am not an expert in pairing food with wine, but I think something bitter, very cold, maybe a little fizzy would be good to wash this cuisine down. Did I just describe a beer? Oh, no!

In the interests of public safety, my final suggestion for petrol station wine is obvious: de-alcoholized wine. Make wine, then remove the alcohol using either reverse osmosis or the "spinning cone" technique. The result isn't exactly wine as most of us normally recognize it, but it looks like wine and serves a purpose. And there's very little chance it will raise your blood-alcohol level in case you are pulled over by the police. Hmmm. I guess it's that "unleaded" wine I said I was going to avoid. Damn!

FAST-FOOD WINE

It is still unusual to find wine available at a fast-food restaurant here in the United States. When I stumbled upon a Burgerville store selling wine outside of Vancouver, Washington, a few years ago, I simply had to give it a try, and the A to Z Oregon Pinot Gris paired very nicely with halibut and chips! Wine is not so unusual in casual-dining settings in other parts of the world, but alcohol regulations here in the United States create a bit of a maze that few fast-food providers are willing to try to navigate. What a pity!

But the fast-food restaurants of my dreams have lots of wine choices—why shouldn't they? But what particular wines? As you can tell, any wine at all would make me happier, but what kind of wine would be best for a burger-and-fries or fish-and-chips joint? Keg wine is the obvious first step. Keg wine doesn't come in bottles or bags but in stainless-steel barrels, and the wine is drawn through a spigot, much like a soda or beer tap. Inert gas keeps the remaining wine from oxidizing. When the process works as planned, the wine can be fresher, cheaper, and even greener than traditional bottle-poured wine by the glass.

Wine kegs would fit in very well with the fast-food environment, and I suspect that when wine really does come to the world of the Big Mac and the Whopper, this is how it will arrive. But what ought to be inside the kegs? That's the bigger challenge for your imagination. It should be sparkling, I suppose, to mimic the traditional soft drinks, and perhaps even served in a paper cup, but that would be too much, wouldn't it? Sparking Shiraz, the Australian specialty, would actually be a great accompaniment to hamburgers, and Lambrusco from Emilia Romagna in Italy, both dry and a bit sweet, would go with almost everything else.

These are good choices, I believe—you can probably think of even better ones—but I admit they are a bit conventional since these wines already exist. An imaginary wine should be something that doesn't exist, perhaps can't exist. So maybe wines that carry the flavors of condiments, such as tomato ketchup, tartar sauce, mustard, or malt vinegar? What strange and exciting flavors they would be! Hot wines—Tabasco sauce or sriracha? And what would be better than if they were fast wines, like the fast foods they are designed to accompany—that were transformed from grape to wine in front of your eyes? Now that would be exciting.

ASTRONAUT WINE

The most unlikely place I can imagine to drink wine is in outer space—on the International Space Station, for example.[7] Alcohol in space is nothing new—I have seen a photo of Russian cosmonauts drinking Cognac on the Mir space station, and I suspect that wine has made an appearance somewhere some-time in earth orbit. I understand that a proposal to add a little Sherry to the US astronaut diet was nixed back in the 1970s—a combination of cost con-cerns, external pressure, and flight-crew disinterest. Too bad—I would love to have seen the tasting note!

Drinking wine in zero gravity would necessarily require some adjust-ment—pouring the precious liquid into a Riedel glass would be the first challenge, and any attempt to swirl and sniff would result in (airborne) wine, wine everywhere (and not a drop to drink). So the first compromise is obvi-ous—use a straw (like one of those kid's juice boxes?) or maybe a sippy-cup, but then some of the aroma notes must be sacrificed. But other than that, the wine should be fine, shouldn't it? Not necessarily, because the environment in orbit is likely to differ by more than the absence of earth's firm pull. The closest thing to space that most of us will experience is drinking wine on an airline flight, and it is well known that wine (and food, too) tastes different at 30,000 feet than it does back at sea level. The food doesn't change, you don't change—or at least not much, apart from perhaps being a bit more tired and stressed. But the atmosphere around you is certainly different.[8] The atmosphere is very dry, for example, which dries out your nasal passages and reduces your sense of smell (memo to self: bring along a purified water in-haler next time). The atmospheric pressure is also reduced, which apparently affects your taste buds in several ways. The perception of acidity is reduced, which means that well-balanced wines may taste flat. And, of course, airplanes are noisy, and that loud background roar also takes its toll on your senses.

Bottom line: subtle flavors and aromas are more difficult to detect at al-titude, and the food and wine specialists at the major airlines go out of their way to amp up the sensory profiles of the food and wine to compensate. Alaska Airlines challenged their wine supplier, Precept Wines, to develop wines custom-tailored to the aircraft environment.[9] The resulting Canoe Ridge Merlot and Pinot Gris wines were tweaked versions of the standard bottlings. The tannic and oak aspects of the Merlot were elevated, and a little Syrah was added to the blend to increase the wine's aromatics. A tiny bit more residual sugar was left in the Pinot Gris to rebalance the impact of the airplane environment on perceived acidity. Why would a winery go to such trouble to make a wine for high-altitude travelers? Money, of course. The travel-related market—airlines, cruise ships, duty-free shops, and so on—is an attractive market for wine sales, and so wineries will go to some trouble to get their wines in the air or on the sea.

Since everyone is different when it comes to these things, I am sure that some people are more affected by noise, pressure, and humidity than others, and I suspect that the differences in how we perceive wine are probably magnified by stratospheric travel. I performed a small and unscientific test on a recent flight from London to Seattle, on which I was fortunate to be sitting in the business-class section. The flight attendants humored me by serving small glasses of all the wines on offer. They were all tasty (someone at British Airways is doing their job), but they were all quite intense—the Old World wines probably fruitier than I might expect in order to compensate for the dulling impact of the airplane environment. I was surprised to find that the wines that I liked best at 38,000 feet were quite different from the ones I would have chosen in a restaurant.

I wonder what wine would taste like in space? Since I can only imagine, let me say that I think it would be delicious, full of moonlight and stars, smelling like a baby's breath, and tasting like mother's milk. What a cosmic experience!

BACK TO THE INVISIBLE CITIES

I could keep going in this vein—the number of imaginary wines is surely much larger than the number of real ones and, as we have seen, that number is very large indeed. But would I really accomplish my goal, which was to elevate and inspire? Astronaut wines are surely elevated in a literal sense, and I do find them just a little inspiring. But I am no Marco Polo, and I fear my ability to imagine is inferior to his. So allow me to circle back to one of my favorite invisible cities in Calvino's book.[10]

"When you have arrived at Phyllis," Marco Polo explains, "you rejoice in observing all the bridges over the canals, each different from the others: cambered, covered, on pillars, on barges, suspended, with tracery balustrades. And what a variety of windows looks down on the streets: mullioned, Moorish, lancer, pointed . . . At every point the city offers surprises to your view."

But this is a stranger's view, the newcomer's perspective. When you are long in Phyllis, the scene changes and the intricate detail fades away. "Millions of eyes look up at the windows, bridges, capers, and they might be scanning a blank page," Marco Polo's story ends. "Many are the cities like Phyllis, which elude the gaze of all, except the man who catches them by surprise." The invisible city seems to disappear before its citizens' eyes. The city is still there, I suppose, it is just that no one sees it anymore. No one really looks. Familiarity doesn't breed contempt so much as apathy.

Is wine a bit like Phyllis? I hope not, but maybe it is impossible to know from the inside. Maybe the citizens of Phyllis don't see what they don't want to see or what they've seen so many times before. If so—and if life and wine are like Phyllis—then there is special reason to treasure Marco Polo's tales, Eric Asimov's rare treasures, and my imaginary wines, whether they really exist or not, since they have the ability to catch us by surprise and to open our eyes, at least for a moment, to the richness that our lives can hold.

What does this have to do with money, taste, and wine? I suppose that it shows that there is more to taste and wine than money and that there are some things that even money cannot buy—but that doesn't mean that we cannot savor them! So is this how the book ends? With an appeal to imagination to resolve the money–taste–wine trilemma? Perhaps! But you won't know for sure until you turn the page and read the final chapter.

Chapter 14

Groot Expectations

The final chapter of any book is the last stop on a journey, and it seems that my books about wine take this notion literally. *Wine Wars* ended with a real journey through Napa Valley, searching for a resolution to the tensions between and among, as the subtitle said, the curse of the Blue Nun, the miracle of Two Buck Chuck, and the revenge of the Terroirists. The last chapter of *Extreme Wine* told the story of my first visit to South Africa. All of the extremes of the wine world that I investigated throughout that book seemed to come together in surprising ways during my short stay in the remote and beautiful Cape Winelands.

Now it is another book and another journey, and although I have covered a lot of territory since our last meeting—I've now explored wine on every continent, except Antarctica—I find myself back in Africa, this time to give a keynote address to a wine-industry group. South Africa feels like the right place to end this journey into the complicated relationship among money, taste, and wine, so humor me and come along for the ride. I want to explain why South Africa inspires me to have groot (great) expectations about how the money, taste, and wine triangle will work itself out.

RETHINKING SOUTH AFRICA AND ITS WINE

Can wine change the world? Or at least the way that we see the world? That's a lot to ask of a simple beverage, even one as ancient and beloved as wine. And yet I think that maybe wine can be an agent of change, and, if I can convince you of this, it will be an interesting way to end our journey. Money, taste, and wine can combine to move the world ahead just a bit?

That's why we are in South Africa. What you think about South Africa and its wines depends on how and when you have been exposed to them in the past. For many people, the country itself is defined by its history of apartheid. When I was at university, the buzz about South Africa was divesting stock holdings in the country as a way to protest apartheid, which understandably left a bad taste in our young mouths. The wine sometimes didn't taste so good either, when we were finally able to sample it a few years later. South African wine was often defined by a first taste of Pinotage, the country's signature grape variety.[1] Some of the inexpensive Pinotage wines that went out in the first wave of exports after the end of apartheid gave both the grape variety and its native land a bad reputation. Those of us of a certain age can be forgiven for not rushing to embrace South Africa and its wines.

But things have changed, both in the country and the wine, and there is much credit to be shared for this. As Nelson Mandela observed, "They always say that time changes things, but you actually have to change them yourself."[2] South African wines are now some of the best in the world, regularly taking home top prizes in the Decanter World Wine Awards competition. South Africa is a country with big problems and great (I almost said groot) potential; it is slowly finding its way in the brave new world Mandela helped open up just a few years ago, and wine is playing a part in the process.

The wine industry group Wines of South Africa (WOSA) released a series of videos in 2014 celebrating the twentieth anniversary of democracy in South Africa.[3] What does democracy have to do with wine? I don't have a general theory yet, unlike my primitive money–taste–wine trilemma theory, but I can tell you that the two are very closely linked when it comes to South Africa. The birth of democracy coincided with the end of apartheid and the closing of the long years of isolation for the country and its wine industry. To a certain extent, South Africa and its wine industry were both reborn two decades ago. Things are much different twenty years on, and WOSA's democracy-themed videos are one way to make the point. Now, as I will try to explain below, a person with ethical concerns might well *seek out* South African wines rather than boycott them. Revolutionary!

Thandi Wines, the subject of the first video in the series, is a good example of how money, taste, wine, and human dignity can all work together. Thandi, which means nurturing love in the Xhosa language, was started in 1995 at the initiative of Paul Cluver. A partnership that includes more than 250 farm-worker families in Elgin, it was the first black economic empowerment project in the agriculture sector and is today one of the most successful of them. In 2003, it became the first fair-trade-certified winery in the world! Thandi's success has been contagious: South Africa now leads the world in fair-trade wine, where some of the profits from wine sales are reserved for community-development projects. My South African friends point out that not all black economic empowerment initiatives in the wine industry have been as successful as Thandi—much is left to do, they say, and more resources are needed. South Africa's social and economic problems are still very large, and I think it is important that wine—one of the country's most visible global industries—is part of the solution.

Thandi is exceptional, but it is far from the only story. One defining element of the new South Africa is called Premium Independent Wineries of South Africa (PIWOSA). What these fourteen wineries have in common, besides their focus on export markets, is a strong set of values and a commitment to quality, which they seek to communicate in defining their niche in the marketplace, and with that they hope to help define South Africa's position, too.

The members of PIWOSA have agreed on an ethics charter that reflects their collective commitment to certain values. The charter defines a set of ethical relationships both in theory and in practice and provides for effective monitoring of behavior, especially worker relationships. Member wineries are also audited for progress toward black economic empowerment goals. Three of the PIWOSA members—Paul Cluver, Jordan (Jardin here in the United States because of trademark considerations), and The Winery of Good Hope—have taken the next step by collaborating on import and distribution in the US market, gaining scale and exploiting their shared goals and diverse products lines. This is the way that money, taste, and wine can work together—to achieve fine wine and social change.

THE ONE-CORK THEORY OF DEVELOPMENT

My friend Aaron Ausland, who works on economic and social development projects around the globe, once told me that he aimed to change the world one diaper at a time. His point was that while a lot of attention is focused on big projects, microinitiatives that change living conditions for even just a few families can have great value when replicated and compounded over time and space. If enough people take small actions and together change enough diapers for a long enough period of time, the theory goes, pretty soon they will have changed the world. It's an idea that inspires even in seemingly hopeless situations, such as the poorest parts of South Africa. Aaron's specialty is microfinance, small loans made to enable the efforts of individual entrepreneurs in low-income areas, and I think you might be able to see how theory and practice come together in his work.

I think of Thandi and PIWOSA as models of what you might call the "one-cork" development theory put into practice for wine, and when we visited the Paul Cluvers (both Dr. Cluver, who founded the winery, and his son, Paul, who now runs it), we saw that there is actually much more to their commitment to social change than just the wine. We attended a children's theater performance at the Hope@Paul Cluver Amphitheater, which is set in a eucalyptus grove on the Cluver farm. The profits from the theater's programs support local efforts to deal with HIV, tuberculosis, and terminal diseases and to care for the children of the stricken. This is just one of several local initiatives that Cluver supports. Do you see the one diaper connection?

We witnessed a number of other modest but worthy one-cork efforts as we toured the Cape Winelands. Even though it is the largest South African export brand in the United States, for example, there is no way that the de Wet family of Excelsior Wine Estate can solve all the economic and social problems in the Robertson region where they are located. So they take small but important steps: resisting mechanization, for example, to preserve farm jobs in a region with high unemployment, and making a serious effort to promote workers into jobs with more responsibility.

We saw this moving-up notion at work when we visited Gary and Kathy Jordan at the Jordan Wine Estate in Stellenbosch. Attention to workers and their conditions was a founding principle at Jordan, where worker housing was built before the owners' own home. Jordan has encouraged farm workers to move up by sponsoring education, including advanced WSET (Wine & Spirit Education Trust) classes, in some cases. Jancis Robinson recently wrote about another innovative Jordan program to provide "South Africa Women in Wine" internship experiences.

Education is obviously a key element of any one-cork program, and we saw winery-worker education initiatives in many places. One of the most striking was at Durbanville Hills winery, which is a partnership between drinks giant Distell and a group of local farmers. Social justice has been a goal from the start for this winery, which formally includes workers in the profit structure and on the managing board. Albert Gerber and Martin Moore took us to a preschool that the winery runs to get the children of farm workers off to a strong start. The winery supports education, paying school tuition and other expenses as far as a child can go in school.

These private, social-change initiatives are supported by an industry-wide commitment that you can actually see when you buy a bottle of South African wine. Almost every bottle of South African wine you are likely to find will bear a seal from the Wine and Spirits board certifying the "Integrity & Sustainability" of its producer or a newer seal that attests to fair-labor practices, too. The idea is to spread ethical behaviors throughout the wine industry, throughout the wine supply chain, and to set a model for South Africa, and perhaps the world. Talk about the power of one-cork development!

There is much left to do, of course, and there is an understandable debate on when, what, and how to move forward. Sometimes it seems like common commitment about what needs to be done is forgotten in disagreements about strategy and tactics. What's important is that the debate does not become divisive, momentum continues to build, and change takes place. Change is what's important, and I guess you have to do it yourself, even if it comes one diaper or cork at a time.

SECOND STAR TO THE RIGHT

"Second star to the right and straight on till morning." These are the directions to Neverland as given by Peter Pan in J. M. Barrie's famous play of the same name.[4] Your final destination is just beyond the horizon—just keep going; you can't miss it. Clear and vague in equal measure. That's just the way I felt halfway through our visit to South Africa. We were in Barrydale in a region called Klein Karoo, there to visit the Joubert family, staying at Helena Joubert's Lentelus B&B and visiting with her multigeneration winemaking family.

The Jouberts have been winemakers in South Africa for generations—the first Joubert was a French Huguenot who came seeking opportunity and religious freedom. The weight of the family's history was tangible when Sue and I followed Cobus Joubert down into the cellar, where a fragile old barrel was stored. The wine, which I first wrote about in *Extreme Wine*, was more than two hundred years old—a sweet Muscat d'Alexandrie made in 1800, or thereabouts. The Jouberts draw out a tiny amount each year and replace it with new wine in a simplified solera system. We'd tasted it before from the bottle, but never directly from the barrel. What a magnificent experience—and what an incredible journey that wine has taken, too.

We returned from a day of winery visits in Robertson to learn that Meyer Joubert had a proposition for us. One of his semiregular customers at Joubert-Tradauw Private Cellar had come into the winery that day and invited him to a "braai"—South Africa's national feast—which you and I would recognize as a kind of barbeque over wood coals, with salads, wine, and good company. Meyer accepted on the condition that his American guests come along, too. And so we grabbed some wine (including a bottle of Lanzerac Pinotage that we had been given), stopped for some meat (boerwoerst sausage and Karoo lamb chops), and took the 4x4 pickup out of town (Sue in the cab with Meyer as I was standing up in the pickup bed with eight-year-old Andreas). We turned off the highway into the bush, following a dirt track that had been washed out in several places. On and on we went into the wilderness—even Meyer, who loves this sort of thing, hadn't been here before.

The sun was setting over the mountains when we arrived at our destination about 7 kilometers into the wilderness. The location was as remote as it was beautiful, and the house was beautiful, too. In fact, it was spectacular, filled with a collection of African art. The owners had purchased 1,000 hectares of land, which they fenced as a private game reserve where they'd try to protect some threatened local animal species. Solar panels and a deep well gave them water and power, and a satellite dish provided video and Internet. It was paradise at the end of the road, or the end of the world, depending on how you look at it.

And so in this scene of great contrasts in a land of even greater contrasts, we built the wood fire and shared a braai with the folks who were there. Strangers before, brought together by the wine and food, we became friends. That's what wine does, after all, that's why we are still making and drinking it after many thousands of years. If it couldn't perform magic like this—bringing together strangers from thousands of miles away and giving them something warm and personal to share—I'm not sure it would still play such a central role in our existence.

I guess it wasn't really magic. It could all be explained quite logically. But it sure seemed like magic as we bounced back to the highway and then Barrydale with Lentelus just beyond, Andreas now asleep inside the truck with Meyer and Sue and me outside, shivering in the truck bed but happy as Tinkerbell to be there. Second star to the right. That was more or less the direction we headed, but it was hard to tell for sure with an ocean of stars above.

JOURNEY'S END

Sometimes you don't really know where a journey will take you, you just set out and see what happens. This book's journey has taken us on a trek through the world of money, taste, and wine. We started out with an undeniable and revolting fact: even though everyone knows it ain't so, we are all so programmed to think that more expensive wines are better than cheaper ones that we can practically taste the money in the wine. Money, taste, and wine are caught in an unhealthy love triangle. Something's got to give.

"Know thyself" was my first piece of advice. Take money away and start to understand your taste for wine. Easier said than done, but it is a beginning. We then progressed through an unlikely lineup of wines—dump bucket, Treasure Island, and big-box. The situation got worse when we considered the identity crisis of wine labels and enlisted in the Restaurant Wars. Like a punch-drunk boxer, sometimes it seemed like taste and wine were on the ropes. But like Rocky in the classic films taste rallied, and by the end, after wine snobs, cheese bores, imaginary wines, and Anything But Champagne, we were able to follow the money to wine investing and then to wine crime. By the time we got to South Africa, my groot expectations looked like a reality. Money, taste, and wine don't just work together, sometimes they can change the world!

Which brings us here, not to Neverland with Peter Pan and the Lost Boys, but to the end of the book. And what have we learned? Lots of little things, I hope, about wine, the wine business, and the complicated relationship that is at the heart of this book, and maybe a few big things, too, about wine and life. To paraphrase a famous soccer coach, wine isn't *like* life, it *is* life, and life is complicated, so I guess wine must be complicated. Perhaps wine lovers are better equipped than most to appreciate wine's many sides (and life's, too) even as like Kublai Khan they search for an ephemeral kernel of truth. *Salut!*

Notes

CHAPTER 1: THE WINE BUYER'S BIGGEST MISTAKE

1. The data shown here are from ratings in the June 30, 2013 issue of *Wine Spectator*.

2. Robin Goldstein, Alexis Herschkowitch, and Tyce Walters, eds., *The Wine Trials 2011* (Dallas: Fearless Critic Media, 2010).

3. Hilke Plassmann, John O'Doherty, Baba Shiv, and Antonio Rangel, "Marketing Action Can Modulate Neural Representations of Experienced Pleasantness," *Proceedings of the National Academy of Sciences* 105, no. 3 (2008): 1050–54.

4. Felix Salmon, "How Money Can Buy Happiness: Wine Edition," Reuters, October 27, 2013.

http://blogs.reuters.com/felix-salmon/2013/10/27/how-money-can-buy-happiness-wine-edition/ (accessed November 14, 2013).

5. Clark Smith, *Postmodern Winemaking* (Berkeley: University of California Press, 2013).

6. I analyzed the geography of the wine wall in my 2011 book, *Wine Wars*.

7. At least this is one of the points that Matt Kramer makes about Gaja's achievement in his valuable book, *Matt Kramer's Making Sense of Italian Wine*

(Philadelphia: Running Press, 2006). I reviewed the many sources of Gaja's success in my 2013 book, *Extreme Wine*; see pages 112–14 there.

CHAPTER 2: ANATOMY OF A COMPLICATED RELATIONSHIP

1. There is actually a brand of wine called *Ménage à Trois*.

2. Robert Mundell is usually given credit for the idea, and I wrote about his trilemma and another one discovered by Harvard's Dani Rodrick in my 2010 book, *Globaloney 2.0*. Mundell's trilemma involves money (the free international movement of capital), domestic economic stability (promoted by an independent central bank), and international economic stability (with a stable or fixed exchange rate). Rodrick's trilemma is related—it's about money, stability, and democracy. Together they paint a picture of a world with several built-in contradictions where money, when consumed in large quantities, is a very dangerous drug.

3. Buttonwood, "Three's a Crowd: The Instability That Stems from Trilemmas," *Economist*, July 5, 2014.

4. *Mondovino*, DVD, directed by Jonathan Nossiter (THINKfilm, 2014). I analyzed this film in my earlier book, *Wine Wars*.

5. Caro Feely, *Grape Expectations* (West Sussex, UK: Summersdale, 2012), and *Saving Our Skins* (West Sussex, UK: Summersdale, 2014).

6. Olivier Magny, *Stuff Parisians Like* (New York: Berkley, 2011).

CHAPTER 3: WINE DRINKER, KNOW THYSELF

1. Karen MacNeil, *The Wine Bible* (New York: Workman, 2000).

2. Jancis Robinson, ed., *The Oxford Companion to Wine*, 3rd ed. (New York: Oxford University Press, 2006).

3. Jancis Robinson, Julia Harding, and José Vouillamoz, *Wine Grapes: A Complete Guide to 1,368 Vine Varieties, Including Their Origins and Flavours* (New York: Ecco/ HarperCollins, 2012).

4. This section is based upon Benjamin Lewin, *Wine Myths and Reality* (Dover, UK: Vendage, 2010). This is another of my favorite wine books—I think of it as a mini Master of Wine course. Lewin is a Master of Wine himself and one of the world's foremost cell biologists.

5. See AromaWheel.com for details.

6. Tim Hanni, *Why You Like the Wines You Like* (Napa, CA: HanniCo, 2013).

CHAPTER 4: DUMP BUCKET WINES

1. For *Sideways* details, please consult the movie's page on the Internet Movie Database website. http://www.imdb.com/title/tt0375063/ (accessed November 19, 2013).

2. *Sideways/Saidoweizu* at the Internet Movie Database. http://www.imdb.com/title/tt1236373/ (accessed November 19, 2013).

3. Rex Pickett, *Vertical* (Santa Monica, CA: Loose Gravel, 2010).

4. Economics textbooks suggest an obvious course—cut price. Lower price will entice old consumers to buy a bit more and new customers to enter your market. Cut price now, and then you can raise it back up once market conditions have returned to normal. It is hard to argue with the logic of this prescription—and it is perfect advice if you are selling a completely homogeneous product like soybeans or corn. Where commodities are homogenous or standardized it makes sense that reputation or brands aren't very important and premium prices are rare. But if your product—your wine or whatever—is different, or at least you want your customers to think so, then a different sort of logic applies, the logic of product differentiation.

5. It can also be an illegal one. International trade agreements forbid dumping from one country into another's market if the sales are made below production cost and if it damages the domestic producers in the process. Why would anyone sell a wine below cost? In some cases that would be better than lowering the price back home in the principal market (especially if you cannot conveniently raise it back again). For economists, the type of dumping makes a difference—one-time foreign sales that give those consumers a once-in-a-lifetime deal aren't as much of a concern as predatory dumping, for example, where the below-cost sale is strategically aimed at driving competitors out of the market. But dumping is dumping, and it is a surprisingly common marketing strategy.

6. The overvalued Australian dollar exchange rate was part of this story, too.

7. See John H. Wright, *Domaine Chandon: The First French-Owned California Sparkling Wine Cellar* (Regional Oral History Office, University of California at Berkeley, Bancroft Library Collection, 1992). http://www.archive.org/stream/

sparklingwinecellar00wrigrich/sparklingwinecellar00wrigrich_djvu.txt (accessed November 20, 2013).

8. Benjamin Lewin, *What Price Bordeaux?* (Dover, UK: Vendage, 2009), see esp. chap. 11, "Grand Vins and Second Wines," 195–209.

CHAPTER 5: TREASURE ISLAND WINES

1. The data in this section is taken from the Costco investor website and was up-to-date at the time of writing. http://phx.corporate-ir.net/phoenix .zhtml?c=83830&p=irol-irhome (accessed January 3, 2014).

2. See the current state map of Total Wine & More stores. http://www.totalwine .com/eng/Store-Locator (accessed February 24, 2014).

3. Bonded wineries actually produce wine for sale and therefore must be "bonded" by tax authorities. In addition to bonded wineries, there are also "virtual" wineries that sell wine and have wine brands, but they do not produce any wine themselves, contracting this out to bonded wineries. Of the total of 7,762 US wineries at the start of 2014, for example, 1,197 were virtual wineries. The largest of these virtual wineries, Castle Rock Winery, sells more than 500,000 cases of wine.

4. Winery historical data provided by Wine Institute. https://www.wineinstitute.org/ resources/statistics/article124 (accessed February 24, 2014).

5. See Cathy Fisher, "Total U.S. Wineries Hits 7,762," *Wine Business Monthly*, February 2014, 82–85, for full details.

6. This is the famous Shipwreck Beads store, with the largest bead selection in the world. http://www.shipwreckbeads.com/ (accessed February 24, 2014).

7. To view the cool graphic showing the constellation of wines and wineries and distributors referred to in the text, please see Phil Howard, Terra Bogart, Alix Grabowski, Rebecca Mino, Nick Molen, and Steve Schultze, "Concentration in the U.S. Wine Industry," Michigan State University, December 2012. https://www.msu .edu/~howardp/wine.html (accessed February 24, 2014).

8. To view the study on the relative diversity of wine selections at different Michigan retainers, see Rebecca Mino, "The Availability of Michigan-Produced Wines in Southern Michigan Retail Locations," Michigan State University, May 2012. https:// www.msu.edu/~howardp/michiganwine.html (accessed February 24, 2014).

CHAPTER 6: SOMETIMES THE BEST WINE IS A BEER (OR A CIDER!)

1. Tom Acitelli, *The Audacity of Hops* (Chicago: Chicago Review Press, 2013).

2. See Max Fisher, "How Jimmy Carter Saved Craft Beer," *The Wire*, August 5, 2010. http://www.thewire.com/entertainment/2010/08/how-jimmy-carter-saved-craft-beer/19195/ (accessed June 4, 2014).

3. Garrett Oliver, ed., *The Oxford Companion to Beer* (New York: Oxford University Press, 2012).

4. See Chris Fumari, "A. C. Nielsen Rep: In Three Years 50,000 New Beer Sellers," *Brewbound*, December 12, 2012. http://www.brewbound.com/news/a-c-nielsen-rep-in-3-years-50000-new-beer-sellers (accessed June 4, 2014).

5. See the product description for Midas Touch and other innovative products on the Dogfish Brewery website. http://www.dogfish.com/brews-spirits/the-brews/year-round-brews/midas-touch.htm (accessed June 4, 2014).

6. This tasting note is taken from a promotional e-mail from a Seattle wine seller ImpulseWine.com; see also details there. http://impulsewine.com/epic-ales/ (accessed August 12, 2014).

7. Most of the cider is made for others and sold under their label—a practice common in the wine industry, too. Production of Blue Mountain Cider was about 20,000 cases in 2014.

8. Sarah Nassauer, "The Real Apple Shortage," *Wall Street Journal*, May 6, 2014. http://online.wsj.com/news/articles/SB10001424052702304101504579546112711323256 (accessed June 4, 2014).

9. See Blandina Costa, "Moscatel de Setúbal Awarded Best Muscat of the World," *Portugal Daily View*, July 12, 2011. http://www.portugaldailyview.com/whats-new/wine-moscatel-de-setubal-awarded-best-muscat-in-2011 (accessed June 5, 2014).

CHAPTER 7: BULK UP

1. See Lauren Eads, "Wine 'Bladder' Bursts into Street," *The Drinks Business*, March 4, 2014. http://www.thedrinksbusiness.com/2014/03/wine-bladder-bursts-onto-street/ (accessed March 28, 2014). Apparently this was not the first traffic-accident–caused-wine flood!

2. I wrote about big-bladder box wine in my earlier book, *Wine Wars.* The subject attracted so much attention that I thought I should expand upon the analysis here.

3. There are several published interviews and profiles of Mr. Scholle. Purdue University has published a very detailed one. https://news.uns.purdue.edu/html3month/030927.Scholle.chair.html (accessed March 28, 2014).

4. The total value of off-premises wine sales in the United States increased by about 4.6 percent in 2013. Box wines come in several sizes—3-liter, 4-liter, and 5-liter—and in different price and quality levels. The market for 5-liter boxes increased by only a little more than 4 percent, and sales of 4-liter boxes actually declined.

5. Three-liter boxes sales have fallen in the UK market because of alcohol-tax increases that have made them much more expensive. Sales of 2.25-liter boxes have risen to take their place. The tax is levied according to the quantity of wine in the container, not the value of the wine, and so has a disproportionate impact on larger container of inexpensive wine.

6. See Michael F. Spatt and Mark L. Feldman, *Grape-A-Hol: How Big Business Is Subverting Artisan Winemaking and the Future of Fine Wine* (Indianapolis, IN: Dog Ear, 2012).

CHAPTER 8: MORE THAN JUST A LABEL

1. Henry Jeffreys, "Should Cats Sell Wine?" on Tim Atkin MW's website. http://www.timatkin.com/articles?1356 (accessed June 2, 2014).

2. Matt Harvey, Leanne White, and Warwick Frost, eds., *Wine and Identity: Branding, Heritage, Terroir* (London: Routledge, 2014).

3. For a complete account of the founding of the winery and the development of the label, see Jeremy Beer, *Organically Sublime, Sustainably Ridiculous: The First Quarter-Century of Frog's Leap* (Kennett Square, PA: Union Street, 2007).

4. See "Moving with the Times," in the *Rabobank Wine Quarterly Outlook for Global and Regional Markets* (Q3, 2014).

5. David Schuemann, *99 Bottles of Wine: The Making of the Contemporary Wine Label* (Napa, CA: Val de Grace, 2013).

6. See ibid., 128–29.

7. Thanks to Susan McEachern for suggesting that I write about wine labels in this book.

CHAPTER 9: WINE SNOBS, CHEESE BORES, AND THE GLOBALIZATION PARADOX

1. Simon Kuper, "An Everyday Taste of Happiness," *Financial Times*, November 29, 2013. http://www.ft.com/intl/cms/s/2/f3f7be5a-56fb-11e3-8cca-00144feabdc0 .html#axzz2m35JVgs3 (accessed December 8, 2013).

2. See "Giving Up the Gosht," *Economist*, October 19, 2013. http://www.economist .com/news/britain/21588077-future-curry-houses-looks-grim-giving-up-gosht (accessed December 8, 2013).

3. Ibid.

4. See "Britain Prime Minister David Cameron Hails Indian Food as Great British Industry," *All India*, November 27, 2013. http://www.ndtv.com/article/india/britain- prime-minister-david-cameron-hails-indian-food-as-great-british-industry-451685 (accessed December 8, 2013).

5. Eric Asimov, "Europeans Stray From the Vine," *New York Times*, November 21, 2013. http://www.nytimes.com/2013/11/27/dining/in-wine-drinking-europe-and- america-trade-places.html/ (accessed December 8, 2013).

6. Tyler Cowen, *Creative Destruction: How Globalization Is Changing the World's Cultures* (Princeton, NJ: Princeton University Press, 2002).

7. George Gale has written a wonderful book about phylloxera, *Dying on the Vine: How Phylloxera Transformed Wine* (Berkeley: University of California Press, 2011).

8. Go to http://www.winecentury.com (accessed December 9, 2013) to test yourself against the list of wine-grape varieties and earn entry into the Century Club if you have tasted widely enough to quality for membership.

9. Kym Anderson and Nanda Aryal, *Where in the World Are Various Wine Grape Varieties Grown? Evidence from a New Database* (Adelaide: University of Adelaide Wine Economics Research Center Working Paper 0213). http://www.adelaide.edu

.au/wine-econ/papers/0213-where-are-wine-grape-varieties-grown-dec2013.pdf (accessed December 9, 2013).

10. Jamie Goode, "Grape Varieties and the Diversity of Wine," *Jamie Goode's Wine Blog*, December 9, 2013. http://www.wineanorak.com/wineblog/uncategorized/ grape-varieties-and-the-diversity-of-wine (accessed December 9, 2013).

CHAPTER 10: ANYTHING BUT CHAMPAGNE

1. Jancis Robinson showed great skepticism about Champagne's special properties in her BBC television series, *Jancis Robinson's Wine Course*.

2. Benjamin Lewin, *Wine Myths and Reality* (Dover, UK: Vendage, 2010).

3. This is the sort of tirade that I studied (and then replicated) in my 2005 book, *Globaloney*.

4. See Jean-Robert Pitte, *Burgundy/Bordeaux: A Vintage Rivalry* (Berkeley: University of California Press, 2008), 39–40.

5. Cold winters sometimes halted fermentation prematurely, and when the bottled wines warmed up in the spring, fermentation continued, and bubbles (and exploding bottles) were one result. Containing the pressure and then systematically perfecting the production process in the first four decades of the nineteenth century gave us the basic wines (and wine business) we know today, but modern Champagnes, even the sweetest ones, are much dryer that those of the past.

6. Search the INAO database yourself. http://www.inao.gouv.fr/public/home. php?pageFromIndex=produits/index.php~mnu=145 (accessed July 20, 1014).

7. John Tagliabue, "Champagne, Switzerland Can't Use Its Own Name" *New York Times*, April 27, 2008.

8. See "Stressed Are the Cheesemakers," *Economist*, July 19, 2014, 29.

9. Kolleen M. Guy, *When Champagne Became French: Wine and the Making of a National Identity* (Baltimore: Johns Hopkins University Press, 2003).

10. Graham Robb, *The Discovery of France* (New York: W. W. Norton, 2007).

CHAPTER 11: RESTAURANT WARS

1. In one season, the chef who was eliminated in the Restaurant Wars was incredibly talented and ultimately triumphed in the final battle, reentering the competition through a secondary set of cooking matches.

2. Dan Ariely, "Choosing the Right Wine for Cheapskates," *Wall Street Journal*, August 15, 2014. http://online.wsj.com/articles/choosing-the-right-wine-for-cheapskates-1408145953 (accessed August 22, 2014).

3. Edmund Osterland, *Wine & the Bottom Line: Restaurant Training Manual* (Washington, D.C.: National Restaurant Association, 1980).

4. Ibid., 11.

5. Ibid.

6. Tyler Colman, "Eataly Vino Turns into a Nutella Bar," *Dr. Vino*, May 8, 2014. http://www.drvino.com/2014/05/08/eataly-vino-nyc-nutella-bar/ (accessed May 12, 2014).

7. Lauren Eads, "Bluffing Brits Know Nothing About Wine," *The Drinks Business*, May 13, 2014. http://www.thedrinksbusiness.com/2014/05/two-thirds-of-brits-know-nothing-about-wine/ (accessed May 12, 2014).

8. Osterland, *Wine & the Bottom Line*, 77.

CHAPTER 12: FOLLOW THE MONEY

1. See William L. Hamilton, "Investing in Wine: Now May Be the Time," *New York Times*, May 20, 2009. http://www.nytimes.com/2009/05/21/business/businessspecial3/21wine.html?emc=eta1&_r=0 (accessed March 17, 2014).

2. "En Primeur Is Dead, Long Live En Primeur," *The Liv-Ex Blog*, May 15, 2014. http://www.blog.liv-ex.com/2014/05/en-primeur-is-dead-long-live-en-primeur.html (accessed July 14 2014). The two losses in the earlier time period were very small, adding to the easy-money allure. The gain in 2008, on the other hand, was more than 100 percent.

3. See Serhan Cevik and Tahsin Saadi Sedik, "A Barrel of Oil or a Bottle of Wine: How Do Global Growth Dynamics Affect Commodity Prices?" *IMF Working Paper* WP/11/1 (January 2011). http://www.imf.org/external/pubs/ft/wp/2011/wp1101.pdf (accessed March 17, 2014).

4. See Michael Veseth, *Selling Globalization* (Boulder, CO: Lynne Rienner, 1998), 82.

5. SoDo stands for "South of the Dome"—the Kingdome sports stadium, in this case, which was demolished by implosion in 2000.

6. See Sarah Jean Green, "Stolen Wine Recovered from Nearby SoDo Storage Site," *Seattle Times*, December 11, 2013. http://seattletimes.com/html/localnews/2022445167_winerecoveredxml.html (accessed March 18, 2014).

7. See Michael Harthorne, "Second Suspect Arrested, Charged in High-End Wine Heist," *KOMO Crime Blotter*, December 10, 2013. http://www.komonews.com/news/crime/Second-suspect-arrested-charged-in-high-end-wine-heist-235266581.html (accessed March 18, 2014).

CHAPTER 13: INVISIBLE CITIES, IMAGINARY WINES

1. Italo Calvino, *Invisible Cities*, trans. William Weaver (New York: Harcourt Brace Jovanovich, 1974). The original Italian edition was published in 1972.

2. Eric Asimov, "Why Can't You Find That Wine," *New York Times*, February 11, 2014. http://www.nytimes.com/2014/02/12/dining/why-cant-you-find-that-wine.html?_r=2 (accessed March 10, 2014).

3. Interestingly, I just discovered that one small-production winemaker in Washington State sells wines under the Eye of the Needle and Haystack brands.

4. Thanks to reader Doug Sloan for this tip. You can find the quote from Ezra Cipes on the Summerhill Pyramid Winery website. http://campaign.r20.constantcontact.com/render?ca=05bec211-6520-4535-8267-9984e998e4de&c=1fa939f0-4c22-11e3-b41b-d4ae5292c426&ch=1fd33020-4c22-11e3-b420-d4ae5292c426 (accessed March 10, 2014).

5. Umberto Eco, *How to Travel with a Salmon and Other Essays*, trans. Diane Sterling and William Weaver (New York: Mariner, 1995).

6. I know of at least one drugstore chain that has its own house brand of wine produced, as a great many retailers do these days. But there is nothing particularly unique about the wine that links it to its pharmacy roots.

7. An interesting article about the history of alcohol in outer space can be found at http://gizmodo.com/why-astronauts-were-banned-from-drinking-wine-in-outer-1513304233 (accessed March 11, 2014).

8. For a good quick summary of the main issues concerning wine taste at altitude, see the article by Joe Roberts, "Why Wine Tastes Differently at Thirty-Five Thousand Feet," at Answers.com. http://wine.answers.com/learn-about-wine/why-wine-tastes-differently-at-thirty-five-thousand-feet (accessed March 11, 2014). Joe Roberts writes about wine on his popular website, 1WineDude.com.

9. Andy Perdue, "Making Wine for High Altitudes," *Wine Business Monthly*, July 2014, 26–31.

10. The descriptions provided here are found in Calvino, *Invisible Cities*, 90–91.

CHAPTER 14: GROOT EXPECTATIONS

1. Pinotage was discovered by a University of Stellenbosch scientist who crossed Pinot Noir (the Pinot part of the name) with Cinsault, which was sometimes called Hermitage hereabouts.

2. I love this quote, which is attributed to Nelson Mandela in one of the *Wines of South Africa* videos, but I cannot find confirmation. It is most often associated with Andy Warhol in the references I have found. Regardless of who said it first, it is a wise observation.

3. You can view the Democracy Series videos on the Wines of South Africa website. http://www.wosa.co.za/democracy_series.php (accessed July 22, 2014).

4. The play appeared in 1904 and was followed by the novel in 1911.

Acknowledgments

I know a lot about debt—I once wrote a book called *Mountains of Debt*—and so let me tell you that there are good debts and bad debts. The difference isn't so much about whether the creditor gets paid back (though that is not a bad thing), but if the debt ends up building something useful that would not otherwise be there. Good debts make us better off, and bad debts just leave a hole in the earth.

I've run up a lot of good debts in the course of writing my books—I literally could not write them without the help and constructive criticism of dozens and dozens of people. In my earlier wine books, I have tried to acknowledge those debts one by one, and the list of creditors has grown to the point where it threatens to overwhelm the book itself. So for *Money, Taste, and Wine*, I have decided to try something different and identify the many organizations and groups of people who've helped move my research.

Thanks first of all to my readers, both those who have read and responded to my earlier books and readers of *The Wine Economist* blog. I can't overstate how many good ideas my readers have provided—and how many bad ideas they have shot down. Then I need to thank all the organizations that have invited me to speak across the United States (in California, Washington, Oregon, Idaho, and Virginia) and around the world (Italy, Portugal, the United Kingdom, Argentina, South Africa, and Australia), letting me get to know new wine people, visit new wine regions, and taste wonderful wines. Thanks also to my audiences big and small, who have been patient and supportive as I have worked out my ideas in front of them.

I owe a huge debt to my global network of wine industry experts, who have given so freely of their time to answer my queries and suggest the real questions that I ought to be asking. I am also grateful to the University of Puget Sound for giving me the opportunity to teach and write about the world of wine.

And then there is my team of loyal "research assistants," who feed me ideas, help me with my crazy experiments, and keep me from going off the rails. It is good to have friends and family, and these people are really special. Thanks for your help and support.

This book did not make itself. I appreciate the expertise and support of the professionals at Rowman & Littlefield who have made it possible: editorial director Susan McEachern, production editor Jehanne Schweitzer, copyeditor Scott Barker, and typesetter Theresa Phillips.

And, finally, the biggest thanks of all (and hugs and kisses, too) to my number-one research assistant and *Wine Economist* contributing editor, Sue Veseth.

Selected Bibliography

Acitelli, Tom. *The Audacity of Hops*. Chicago: Chicago Review Press, 2013.

Anderson, Kym, and Nanda Aryal, *Where in the World Are Various Wine Grape Varieties Grown? Evidence from a New Database*. Adelaide: University of Adelaide Wine Economics Research Center Working Paper 0213.

Asimov, Eric. "Europeans Stray from the Vine." *New York Times*, November 21, 2013.

———. "Why Can't You Find That Wine." *New York Times*, February 11, 2014.

Beer, Jeremy. *Organically Sublime, Sustainable Ridiculous: The First Quarter-Century of Frog's Leap*. Kennett Square, PA: Union Street, 2007.

Buttonwood, "Three's a Crowd: The Instability That Stems from Trilemmas." *Economist*, July 5, 2014.

Calvino, Italo. *Invisible Cities*. Translated by William Weaver. New York: Harcourt Brace Jovanovich, 1974.

Cevik, Serhan, and Tahsin Saadi Sedik. "A Barrel of Oil or a Bottle of Wine: How Do Global Growth Dynamics Affect Commodity Prices?" *IMF Working Paper* WP/11/1 (January 2011).

Cowen, Tyler. *Creative Destruction: How Globalization Is Changing the World's Cultures*. Princeton NJ: Princeton University Press, 2002.

Eads, Lauren. "Bluffing Brits Know Nothing about Wine." *The Drinks Business*, May 13, 2014. http://www.thedrinksbusiness.com/2014/05/two-thirds-of-brits-know-nothing-about-wine/ (accessed May 12, 2014).

Feely, Caro. *Grape Expectations*. West Sussex, UK: Summersdale, 2012.

Gale, George. *Dying on the Vine: How Phylloxera Transformed Wine*. Berkeley: University of California Press, 2011.

Goldstein, Robin, Alexis Herschkowitch, and Tyce Walters, eds. *The Wine Trials 2011*. New York: Fearless Critic Media, 2010.

Guy, Kolleen M. *When Champagne Became French: Wine and the Making of a National Identity*. Baltimore: Johns Hopkins University Press, 2003.

Hamilton, William L. "Investing in Wine: Now May Be the Time." *New York Times*, May 20, 2009.

Hanni, Tim. *Why You Like The Wines You Like*. Napa, CA: HanniCo, 2013.

Harvey, Matt, Leanne White, and Warwick Frost, eds. *Wine and Identity: Branding, Heritage, Terroir*. London: Routledge, 2014.

Kuper, Simon. "An Everyday Taste of Happiness." *Financial Times*, November 29, 2013.

Lewin, Benjamin. *What Price Bordeaux?* Dover, UK: Vendage, 2009.

———. *Wine Myths and Reality*. Dover, UK: Vendage, 2010.

Magny, Olivier. *Stuff Parisians Like*. New York: Berkley, 2011.

Nassauer, Sarah. "The Real Apple Shortage." *Wall Street Journal*, May 6, 2014.

Osterland, Edmund. *Wine & the Bottom Line: Restaurant Training Manual*. Washington, D.C.: National Restaurant Association, 1980.

Pitte, Jean-Robert. *Burgundy/Bordeaux: A Vintage Rivalry*. Berkeley: University of California Press, 2008.

Plassmann, Hilke, John O'Doherty, Baba Shiv, and Antonio Rangel. "Marketing Action Can Modulate Neural Representations of Experienced Pleasantness." *Proceedings of the National Academy of Sciences* 105, no. 3 (2008): 1050–54.

Robb, Graham. *The Discovery of France: A Historical Geography from the Revolution to the First World War*. New York: W. W. Norton, 2007.

Robinson, Jancis, Julia Harding, and José Vouillamoz. *Wine Grapes: A Complete Guide to 1,368 Vine Varieties, Including Their Origins and Flavours.* New York: Ecco/HarperCollins, 2012.

Salmon, Felix. "How Money Can Buy Happiness: Wine Edition." Reuters, October 27,

2013. http://blogs.reuters.com/felix-salmon/2013/10/27/how-money-can-buy-happiness-wine-edition/ (accessed November 14, 2013).

Schuemann, David. *99 Bottles of Wine: The Making of the Contemporary Wine Label.* Napa, CA: Val de Grace, 2013.

Smith, Clark. *Postmodern Winemaking.* Berkeley: University of California Press, 2013.

Spatt, Michael F., and Mark L. Feldman, *Grape-A-Hol: How Big Business Is Subverting Artisan Winemaking and the Future of Fine Wine.* Indianapolis, IN: Dog Ear, 2012.

Veseth, Mike. *Extreme Wine.* Lanham, MD: Rowman & Littlefield, 2013.

———. *Wine Wars.* Lanham, MD: Rowman & Littlefield, 2011.

Wright, John H. *Domaine Chandon: The First French-Owned California Sparkling Wine Cellar.* Regional Oral History Office, University of California at Berkeley, Bancroft Library Collection, 1992.

Index

About the Author

Mike Veseth is an economist who studies global wine markets. He is editor of *The Wine Economist* blog and author of a dozen books, including *Extreme Wine* (2013) and *Wine Wars*, which was named a 2011 Wine Book of the Year by JancisRobinson.com. Mike is professor emeritus of International Political Economy at the University of Puget Sound in Tacoma, Washington. He's currently working on his next book, *Around the World in 80 Wines*, when he isn't actually traveling around the world with his wife, Sue, speaking at wine industry conferences, and looking for great wines and great wine stories.